INTERCITY
BUS LINES
OF THE
SOUTHWEST

NUMBER TWENTY-NINE:
The Centennial Series
of the Association of Former Students,
Texas A&M University

INTERCITY BUS LINES OF THE SOUTHWEST

A Photographic History by Jack Rhodes

TEXAS A&M UNIVERSITY PRESS
COLLEGE STATION

Copyright © 1988 by Jack Rhodes
All rights reserved
Manufactured in the United States of America
First Edition Paperback

The paper used in this book meets the minimum requirements of the American National Standard for Permanence of Paper for Printed Library Materials, Z39.48–1984. Binding materials have been chosen for durability.

LIBRARY OF CONGRESS CATALOGING-IN-PUBLICATION DATA

Rhodes, Jack.
   Intercity bus lines of the Southwest.
   (Centennial series of the Association of Former Students ; 29)
   Bibliography: p.
   Includes index.
   1. Bus lines—Southwestern States—History.
I. Title. II. Series: Centennial series of the Association of Former Students, Texas A&M University ; no. 29.
HE5632.S685R46   1988   388.3′22′0976   88-2207
ISBN 0-89096-374-6 (alk. paper)

ISBN 1-58544-015-9 (pbk.)

Buses have been the neglected form of transportation in America. Few except their operators and their customers paid them any mind or attention. Songs were seldom written about them, love was seldom fallen in aboard them, gunmen seldom hijacked them.

But that may be changing. There are signs of new interest in those motorcoaches that ply the roads in search of passengers and express, color and glamour. It's begun with a discovery of its history, with the stories of its pioneers who took old touring cars and their dreams and started bus lines in the early 1900s. It was a hazardous business that required as much in gambling instincts as it did in business sense.

Jack Rhodes has made a significant contribution to that history with this book about the origins of the intercity bus business in Texas and its neighboring states. He tells the stories of the people who started it all. They are the stories that led to the Trailways and the Greyhounds of today. They are stories of visionaries with spirit and grit.

—Jim Lehrer

Contents

List of Illustrations		ix
Acknowledgments		xiii
One.	From the Beginnings to Regulation	3
Two.	The Era of Regulation and Organization	15
Three.	The Depression and the Coming of the War	45
Four.	The War and the Postwar Transition	70
Five.	The Bus Lines of Oklahoma	98
Six.	The Bus Lines of New Mexico	118
Notes		135
Bibliography		145
Index		150

Illustrations

Texas' first intercity bus	4
W. B. Chenoweth	5
Fageol buses	9
Tractor-trailer bus	10
Sun Set Stages, West Texas Coaches	11
Baldwin Motor Co. Studebakers, ca. 1925–26	12
Nunnelee fleet Studebakers	13
Will bus, early 1930s	19
Southland–Red Ball advertisement	20
R. C. Bowen	21
Letter hiring TBOA executive J. C. Carrington	25
Converting buses for passenger service	27
New San Antonio terminal, 1929	33
Loading buses in San Antonio	34
San Antonio society figures boarding coach	35
TBOA transportation to convention	36
Railroad influence on coach design	40
Parlor observation coach, ca. 1930	44
Air-to-bus transfer	46
Touring buses in McAllen, 1931	48
Pickwick-Greyhound "Nite Coach"	51
Fitzjohn sedans	54
Streamlined styling	55
Kerrville "Special," 1930	56
Austin Greyhound terminal, 1939	57
Painter coach in Uvalde, 1937	58
Airline Motor Coaches staff, ca. 1936	59
Streamlined White-Bender model	61
Missouri Pacific Studebaker in Brownsville, 1931	63
Texas Bus Lines "hybrid" coach, 1940	66
Last-of-a-kind Twin Coach model, 1938	67
Beaumont–Port Arthur Bus Line schedule, 1938–39	68
Flxible coach, 1941	71
Arrow Coach Lines' Flxible, 1944	72

Utilitarian wartime coach	74
Wartime Bowen coach	76
Troop movement by bus	77
Clarence Roberson's carved clipboard	78
Car-bus accident	80
Bowen coach, 1942	81
Bowen coach interior	82
Trailer bus in wartime use	84
Kerrville twin-level cruiser, late 1940s	86
Postwar Flxible, 1947	87
Brenham terminal, 1946	88
Six T N M and O Clippers	89
Air-conditioned coach, 1940	90
Painter coach, 1948	91
Small Kemp coach	93
Utilitarian Mooney coach	94
J. C. Carrington	95
Guy Griggs	96
Howard Wesley Allen, 1925	101
Makeshift Allen coach	102
Reo buses in Oklahoma City, ca. 1925–28	103
M K and O garage, 1928	104
M K and O coaches on college field trip	105
M K and O annual dinner, ca. 1939–40	106
Varied fleet of M K and O bus models, 1929	107
Tulsa bus "station," late 1920s	108
M K and O ad poster, late 1930s	109
M K and O Trailways #57	110
Driver Tom Amick, 1925	111
Driver Pinky Carson, 1941	112
Santa Fe Trail Stages	113
Eighteen-passenger Flxibles, 1941	114
Top-of-the-line coaches, 1941	115
Thirty-seven-passenger model, 1941	116
Harveycar at Santa Fe, 1926	119
Harveycar at Tesuque Pueblo, 1926	120
Harveycar on the Indian Detour	121
Harveycar at the Apache Inn	122
Kenworth model coach, 1938	126
Sixteen-passenger Inter City Transit coach	127
Paul McCutchen	128
White Line coach	129

New Mexico Transportation coach at White Sands 130
White model, with emergency exit 131
NMTC coach with Greyhound logo 132
Roswell terminal 133

Acknowledgments

I have been interested in the intercity bus lines of Texas since my childhood in Brownwood and San Antonio, Texas, and Lawton, Oklahoma. Buses have long connoted for me the excitement of travel and the adventure of the open road. While slower and less glamorous than airplanes, steamships, and railroads, motorbuses nevertheless hold a certain appeal for those who deem travel a pleasant and restorative experience.

Beyond this personal affection for the bus lines and the spirit of adventure they represent, I have long felt that those interested in business and transportation history in Texas, Oklahoma, and New Mexico might welcome a pictorial work sketching the development of bus lines in the region. The intercity buses played a significant role in the travel patterns of Texans and other southwesterners during the first half of the twentieth century, but the history of these companies is for the most part not well documented. I hope this brief account will help fill the void.

Many people have contributed toward this book: "bus people," librarians, archivists, staff members of the Railroad Commission of Texas, editors, program planners, photographers, and other people who share an interest in the project. While this list is not exhaustive, I must express my deepest thanks to a number of people, many of whom, unfortunately, died before this history could become a reality.

I could not have written this book without the assistance of John P. Hoschek, editor of *Motor Coach Age* and curator of the Motor Bus Society Library in West Trenton, New Jersey. My greatest indebtedness is to him and his staff.

I must also single out Mr. Joe C. Carrington, the original secretary-manager of the Texas Bus Owners Association, who provided valuable information, original materials, and photographs. His superb secretary, Gladys McCarty Shearer, has taken a personal interest in this book and has continued since Mr. Carrington's death in 1983 to provide invaluable assistance. The support of Joe C. Carrington's family is also gratefully acknowledged.

Countless "bus people"—owners, drivers, ticket agents, clerks, and maintenance people—have supplied anecdotes, reminiscences, and bits of information for this history. All have been generous and forthcoming. Among those going far out of their way over the years to help on the Texas materials have been Alice Roberson Cofer and W. A. "Bill" Lee of Arrow Coach Lines; G. W. "Bill" Hyde and Paul A. Smith of Central Texas Bus Lines; Guy Griggs, John Mosty, Henry Mathews, and J. D. Mahaffey of the Kerrville Bus Company; Tricia Barnett of Continental Trailways; W. L., Sue, Bill, Mary, and Pat Murphey of Sun Set Stages; Lester Welch, Welch Motor Coaches; and Dillard A. Toliver, Farmer Bus Line. For information on New Mexico I am especially indebted to Pat Fuqua of the New Mexico Transportation Company. The "bus people" of Oklahoma supplying special services for this volume include J. T. McMenis and Clarence Starts of the Oklahoma Transportation Company and, at M K and O Lines, John M. Allen, Tom Amick, W. P. Carson, and Herbert Franklin.

During the years of research and interviews leading to this history I encountered a host of helpful research assistants and librarians. All were uniformly professional and accommodating, but several went far beyond the call of duty in assembling materials for this volume. These include Tom Shelton of the University of Texas Institute of Texan Cultures at San Antonio; Kent Middleton and Frances Moore of the Austin Public Library; Kay Dorman of the State Library of New Mexico in Santa Fe; and David B. Gracy, former director of the Texas State Archives in Austin.

For invaluable assistance at the offices of the Railroad Commission of Texas, I am indebted to Walter H. Wendlandt, who was acting director of the Transportation Division during most of my field research in the files, and to Rory K. McGinty, assistant director. Their staff was most cooperative in the retrieval of difficult and often obscure information.

Other historians and bus enthusiasts have encouraged me along the way and have given generously of their advice on this project. Foremost among them is Jim Lehrer of Washington, D.C., who has been a particular source of inspiration. Especially helpful Texas historians include Tom K. Barton of the Colorado College, William Childs of the University of Georgia, L. Tuffly Ellis of the University of Texas at Austin, and Crystal Sasse Ragsdale of New Braunfels.

Reproduction and developing of the photographs used in the book have primarily been the work of Richard Menzies of Salt Lake City, Utah. Mr. Menzies has worked darkroom miracles in getting some photographs of very dubious quality into publishable form. Additional excellent photographic services have been provided by John P. Hoschek of the Motor Bus Society, Stan Kearl of Austin, and Paul Schult of Oxford, Ohio.

While I was on its faculty, the University of Utah provided financial support for this project in the form of travel funds, and for this assistance I am indeed grateful. I have received valuable advice and encouragement also from my colleagues at California State University–Fresno and here at Miami of Ohio.

I am indebted to Janet Lowitz for careful and painstaking attention to the preparation of the manuscript.

Finally, let me acknowledge the affection and assistance supplied during the years of work on this book by my wife, Glenda, who is my best friend and counselor.

INTERCITY
BUS LINES
OF THE
SOUTHWEST

1. From the Beginnings to Regulation

It was about 9:00 P.M. on Monday, October 29, 1907, when W. B. Chenoweth drove his self-designed, six-cylinder "motor driven stage coach" into downtown Snyder, Texas, and thus inaugurated the era of intercity bus travel in the southwestern United States. According to reports of the day, a great number of Snyder's citizens turned out to see the strange contraption, which had just carried a few daring passengers from nearby Colorado City. The trip took these pioneers of motorbus travel all day, since there were numerous breakdowns and no definable roads. Chenoweth reportedly could not secure any passengers for the return trip to Colorado City until he conceived the idea of offering the return ride for free. The next day the bus returned from Snyder to Colorado City with five volunteers lured by that offer of free transportation.[1]

The passengers were not the only ones who were skeptical. Cheoweth had received a scathing reply just eight years previously, when he had written to the National Engineering Laboratory of Philadelphia for a scientific opinion about his six-cylinder, gasoline-fueled engine. In its response of October 18, 1899, the laboratory told the young inventor that he "must have been kicked in the head by a mule when a small boy," which had left him "laboring under the hallucination or delusion that ice could be frozen on a red hot stove by thinking of driving a self-propelled vehicle over a public road 25 miles per hour."[2] This blistering reply, however, did not keep Chenoweth from building his machine. He secured Texas Automobile License Number One for a fee of fifty cents at the Scurry County Courthouse in Snyder on July 12, 1907, and proceeded to found the Texas intercity bus industry that October.

Chenoweth's intercity bus line did not survive long. Passengers were afraid to ride in the noisy, uncomfort-

W. B. Chenoweth is at the wheel of his own invention, a six-cylinder, gasoline-powered "stage coach," the first intercity bus in Texas. Daughters of the Republic of Texas Library at the Alamo.

able, dusty coach, which featured right-hand drive, solid tires, and no muffler. After several unsuccessful months of operation, Chenoweth shifted his efforts to a line running from Big Spring to Lamesa and placed an additional, nearly identical coach in service on that route. As passenger resistance faded and business improved, however, this new venture began to attract competition. A local cattleman bought four Buicks and went into direct competition with Chenoweth. The Buicks were more comfortable and made the trip more speedily, and Chenoweth's venture failed once again. After a similar fate befell his Snyder-to-Roscoe operation, Chenoweth sold his prized inventions to a Fort Worth dairy to be used as trucks. He then left the intercity bus industry for good.

The notion that W. B. Chenoweth had implanted, however, remained in the minds of businessmen and entrepreneurs in Texas and throughout the Southwest. There seemed to be money to be made in the intercity transportation of passengers and freight, especially in areas where rail service was sparse or nonexistent. The motorcar was coming into its own and its skeptics were overcoming their fears of it. Cars and coaches could augment

W. B. Chenoweth about 1940. The "father" of intercity bus service in Texas never achieved long-term success in the industry. Vivian Chenoweth Thacker/University of Texas Institute of Texan Cultures at San Antonio.

the existing rail network by linking rail passenger lines. The new motorized vehicles would be attractive to passengers and shoppers because they could in many cases significantly reduce the time needed to cover the distance. Even in Chenoweth's second experiment, for instance, the coaches on the Lamesa–Big Spring line covered the fifty-five miles in about nine hours instead of the fifteen hours required for the same trip by horse-drawn stagecoach.[3]

The history of the intercity bus industry in Texas, then, is the story of how these entrepreneurs, inventors, businessmen, and ranchers saw economic opportunities in this new mode of transportation and how they went about realizing their dreams. Many were to enter the bus business by accident; a few, by inheritance; others, through a related industry; and still others, through mere curiosity. Theirs is a colorful story, punctuated by fierce competition, sudden business reverses, aggravating highway conditions, quarrels with the giant railroads, and emergency situations created by a depression and two world wars.

As "Dad" Chenoweth had discovered when the four Buicks forced his two "motor-driven stage coaches" out of business between Big Spring and Lamesa, the pioneer era before regulation of the intercity bus industry in Texas was a rough-and-tumble world of no-holds-barred competition. Chenoweth's 1907 venture was twenty years ahead of the imposition of regulation in Texas and some twenty-eight years ahead of federal control through the Interstate Commerce Commission. The period before regulation would see many fledgling bus lines and optimistic owners follow Chenoweth's pattern of invention, expansion, and retreat. Fortunes were made and lost as enterprising pioneers tried to find out where the public wanted to go and then tried to get that same public to use their bus lines to get there.

According to all available records and the memories of those involved, the first regularly scheduled, successfully maintained, and more or less "permanent" intercity bus line began operations in Texas between Luling and San Marcos on March 1, 1912.[4] The operator of this line was a Fentress native named G. J. (Josh) Merritt, who had tried his hand at farming and real estate before purchasing a 1906 Packard and converting it to accommodate seven passengers and their luggage. The Luling–San Marcos line evidently served as something of a shuttle between railroad connections: salesmen coming by train from Houston via the Southern Pacific could change to Merritt's Packard at Luling and ride to San Marcos or the small farming communities between without having to go into San Antonio for a rail transfer to the Katy or the Missouri Pacific; those coming south from Austin or Dallas could transfer at San Marcos for Fentress or Luling. Merritt succeeded with his Luling–San Marcos line and expanded until his operations at one time included Austin to Gonzales and Lockhart to Luling. In 1930 he was still operating a line from Lockhart to San Marcos and had moved into Lockhart, having sold his other franchises to what is now the Kerrville Bus Company.[5]

Few records exist of intercity bus operations in Texas before World War I, and efficient recordkeeping came only after regulation began in 1927. The period before and during the war was characterized by individual operators "testing the waters" of the bus business. A typical pattern was that a young man would have indifferent success—or outright failure—in a related industry such as garage operations or the railroad business and would then see an opportunity in founding a local bus line. Several fledgling companies grew out of local taxi or jitney services, as the drivers and entrepreneurs attempted to convert their routes and cars from local to intercity service.

A fairly representative example occurred far outside of Texas in snowy Minnesota, when Carl Eric Wickman abandoned his Hupmobile dealership and, in 1914, began the service between Alice and Hibbing, which gave rise to Greyhound Lines. By 1916, with the Mesaba iron mines operating at full capacity and more and more miners riding the Mesaba Transportation Company to work, Wickman and his partner, Andy Anderson, were making sixteen thousand dollars' profit on their bus line.[6] In a few years Greyhound Lines would be a major competitor in the bus business in faraway Texas.

Louis Hardy Creamer, a native of Comanche, Texas, followed a pattern similar to Wickman's during the prewar period. During his years as a road builder, Creamer saw the chance to make some money by using the roadways to provide service to the traveling public. He began to drive between Llano and San Saba in 1915 and provided continuous service on that route for more than six years before leaving to build more roads in New Mexico in 1922. Several years later, after he returned to Texas to operate the Creamer Stage Line from Eastland to San Antonio, he reflected on the early days of the Texas bus lines: "The funny part of the bus business is that there seems to be some unusual attraction to it, and it is so fascinating once you get into it that you can hardly get away from it. The funny experiences and the gamble there is to it keeps a feller wondering how and where he will come out, if ever."[7]

One of the variables that caused Creamer to wonder "how and where he will come out" was, of course, the condition of the roads during this formative period. As a road builder himself, Creamer was aware of the deplorable conditions in some areas of the state and of the efforts to improve the public highways.

On the national scene, the establishment of the Office of Public Road Inquiry in 1893 served as a milestone in the phenomenon known as the "Good Roads Movement." The advent of free rural mail delivery near the turn of the century had alerted the public to the need for improved roads, and the development of the automobile probably hastened the growth of the movement. After some years of wrangling between the burgeoning automobile interests, who favored by-passes and high speed roads, and the promoters of farm-to-market roads for the agrarian sector, the federal government produced the Federal Highway Act in July of 1916. The legislation, authored by Sen. John Bankhead of Alabama, introduced in the House of Representatives by Cong. Dorsey Shackleford of Missouri, and passed at the urging of President Woodrow Wilson, attempted to reconcile the interests of both concerns. Additions to the bill in 1921 (restricting federal funds to roads that would subsequently form transcontinental highways) and in 1936 (restoring federal aid to rural and secondary routes) completed the framework of the government legislation that supported the bus lines in most of the period covered by this book.[8]

After World War I: The Growth Years

Immediately after World War I, the discovery of the oil fields near Ranger, Breckenridge, Eastland, Desdemona, and Mexia in Texas sparked new interest in the bus business. The sprawling fields with their wide-open towns lured all manner of adventurers, oil-field workers, camp followers, merchants, relatives, and whole families to the boom areas. Some of these boom towns were several miles from the railroad and offered particularly lucrative opportunities to the bus operators who could get there first.

One such industrious pioneer was Ed Abbott, who had farmed near Snyder until ruined by a drought. During the war Abbott drove a "service car" around Snyder, but in 1918 found himself attracted by the wealth of the oil fields and opened a line from Breckenridge to Eastland.

Four Fageol buses of the Galveston and Houston Auto Transportation Company on charter in West Texas. Best available evidence dates this photograph about 1923. Note the individual doors leading to separate rows of seats; the center aisle had not yet come into use. Motor Bus Society.

It took him five hours to cover the thirty miles between the two towns and he had to locate his own roads because the routes were mostly unmarked at the time.[9] The charge for Abbott's service was five dollars one way, or one dollar per hour of transportation.

Abbott's first advertising was done with a piece of chalk, with which he wrote on the side of his car such notices as "Leave for Breckenridge at 2 PM—$5.00." He was one of the first operators to look into establishing regular schedules and had cards printed announcing the exact hours he intended to leave Eastland and Breckenridge. By 1920, however, the railroads had extended their lines to Breckenridge, and the heyday of Abbott's company was over. He subsequently moved to Lubbock and began a line from Lubbock to Crosbyton.[10]

Another pioneer who got his start during the oil boom was Clarence E. Roberson, who returned from driving an ambulance with the 90th Division in France and Ger-

A Mack chassis served as the basis for this unusual rig from the early 1920s. Texas Oil transported its employees in the Houston–Texas City–Galveston area in this tractor-and-trailer vehicle. There is no evidence that it was ever placed into regular intercity service. Motor Bus Society.

many to find Central Texas booming with oil business. Roberson bought a car on time and started an operation "anywhere people want to go out of Stephenville."[11] He next spent some time serving passengers in the Breckenridge and Desdemona fields, until business there calmed down. He then accepted the invitation of his brother, A. V., to join him in operating buses on a regular schedule between Stephenville and Fort Worth. Clarence Roberson initiated his own service on this popular route on August 8, 1921, and promptly extended his lines to include Brownwood, Waco, Lampasas, Hamilton, and Glen Rose, thus forming the nucleus of an organization later to be known as Arrow Coach Lines.[12] Like most other operators of the day, Roberson served as owner, manager, driver, mechanic, bookkeeper, and general roustabout for the line.

The vehicles of Sun Set Stages, West Texas Coaches, and other carriers load passengers and freight on Main Street in Ballinger in the late 1920s. Sun Set Stages.

The oil fields at Ranger provided the impetus for the entry into the bus business of W. L. Murphey, who drove a service car around Ranger immediately following World War I. He joined his father, O. C., in the family business known as Sun Set Stages, with headquarters in Abilene.[13] According to articles written in O. C. Murphey's own hand and filed with the Texas Railroad Commission at the time of regulation in 1927, the company "began operating regular schedules over this route [from Abilene to Ballinger via Winters] on August 15, 1923." This report to the Railroad Commission called for a fleet of seven cars to be operated, "four as regulars and three as extras."[14] Many other operators, among them W. E. Freeman of Mexia and P. R. "Speedy" Veal on the Texas-Oklahoma border, followed the pattern of Abbott, Roberson, and Murphey in extending operations that they had begun while driving service cars and working the oil fields.

Walter E. Nunnelee was a particularly successful operator in the oil fields of East Texas. After leaving the grocery business in 1916, Nunnelee began jitney and taxi operations in the fields near Tyler and inaugurated regular bus service connecting Tyler, Marshall, and Longview on September 8, 1922. When regulation came to Texas in 1927, Nunnelee was issued Certificate Number One on his line from Tyler to Marshall. He was operating

The Studebakers here assembled in front of the Baldwin Motor Company in Tyler appear to be of 1925-26 vintage. Note the lettering on the lower half of the windshield: "W. E. Nunnelee Auto Line—Tyler Longview and Marshall." W. E. Nunnelee is at the left. Motor Bus Society.

twenty-five coaches when he sold out to a subsidiary of the Cotton Belt Railroad in November, 1928.

One of the most durable and enterprising of these postwar operators was George Wellington Hyde, who was persuaded to enter the jitney business in the Mexia fields in 1921. Hyde was born near Stamford on March 2, 1888, but his family soon moved to Hill County. He enlisted from Cleburne and served in France until his discharge from the Army of Occupation in 1919. After he decided to operate the jitneys, he purchased two Model T's (1918 and 1919 models) for a down payment of $350 and a promise to pay Fort Worth automobile man C. J. Bender $50 a month for seven more months. His business prospered so well that Hyde not only made his payments but also was able to purchase four more Model T's within the first four months of operation. He consistently kept five

As vehicles were added to the Nunnelee fleet, the equipment became more sophisticated and the name changed from "Auto Line" to "Bus Line." Note the covered luggage racks and the increased passenger capacity of these Studebaker fleet additions. Motor Bus Society.

jitneys in service as long as the oil field business flourished. After its demise he journeyed to Dallas, purchased a seven-passenger Cadillac, and started to run a jitney service between Dallas and Fort Worth. This service led to his interest in consolidating with other carriers into the Red Ball Stage Line, which was an amalgamation of outfits called Red Star Lines and Black Diamond Lines.[15]

Small operators like Hyde were at this time starting to band together to face the competition from both wildcatters and larger carriers, because the intercity motorbus industry was reaching the point at which regulation seemed both necessary and inevitable. A contemporary description of the state of the industry illustrates the need for regulation and for bringing order out of the chaos: "Anyone who could make a car run could offer his services for hire. The good runs were often crowded to death, and competition frequently turned into the cut-throat type, with service car operators carrying passengers for cost or less. Often after a good run was established and considerable good will built up, another operator would hop on the route and try to freeze out the original car owner."[16]

As the larger companies developed and expanded their routes, they too became difficult competition for the pioneer bus operators, who frequently saw mergers and alliances as the best defense in a volatile market: "The better routes were taken fast. Often more than one line operated over the same highway, and competition for traffic was intense. The worst part of the situation was that irresponsible drivers would start a service on the sections of the route that offered the cream of the run and would cut the profit out for the companies who made the full run and carried insurance for the protection of their passengers."[17] By the mid-twenties regulation was clearly, and by general consensus, an idea whose time had come.

2. The Era of Regulation and Organization

With the majority of bus line owners seeking regulation and protection of their businesses, the fortieth session of the Texas legislature responded in 1927 by passing a Motor Bus Law.[1] The principal author of the bill, Rep. Walter H. Beck of Fort Worth, recognized the need for regulation and for an orderly administration of the Texas bus industry. Although other legislators, notably J. C. Duvall of Fort Worth, also rigorously supported the legislation, the act quickly became known as the Beck Bus Law, in honor of its author.[2]

The Beck Bus Law became effective June 15, 1927, some eight years before national regulation of the bus lines through the Interstate Commerce Commission. The act gave authority over the bus lines to the Railroad Commission of Texas (RCT), which immediately organized a Motor Transportation Division, with Mark Marshall as the first director.

The Beck Bus Law of 1927 remains an impressive document, despite the relaxation of bus regulations across the United States following the deregulation movements of the Carter administration. For the first time Texas had a definition of motor carriers and their responsibilities and rights. Operators were assured, under terms of the law, that their compliance would protect their franchises and their exclusive rights to haul passengers and freight over a given route. No longer could a bona-fide existing carrier like W. B. Chenoweth be driven out of business by wildcatters and unscrupulous competitors. At the same time, the operators became responsible to an agency of the state government, which could protect not only their interests but also those of their passengers. The law required that the companies provide adequate insurance for both the property and personal safety of their passengers as well as workman's compensation for their employees. It also gave the commission authority to regulate fares and schedules, prescribe and adopt routes, and "supervise and regulate motor bus companies in all other matters affecting the relationship between such motor bus companies and the traveling public that may be necessary to the efficient operation of this law."[3]

One of the strongest weapons of authority granted to the Motor Transportation Division was the sole power to issue Certificates of Convenience and Necessity, which became the instruments popularly known by bus people as "franchises," to operate over routes approved by the Railroad Commission. It was illegal to operate a route without a franchise, and the bill and subsequent amendments provided sanctions against wildcatters who attempted to do so.

The section of the law covering Certificates of Convenience and Necessity contained, however, a grandfather clause that made January 11, 1927, an extremely important date to Texas bus operators. The legislature stated in this section that a temporary certificate or franchise would be issued to a company "when it appears to the satisfaction of the Commission that any motor bus company making application for a certificate or permit is operating and has been continuously operating a motor propelled passenger vehicle service in good faith, over the particular highways designated in said application for certificate or permit, for a period commencing January 11, 1927, or prior thereto."[4]

The law went on to say that such temporary permits "shall become permanent without notice and hearing before the Commission unless a protest shall be filed with the Commission as provided herein."[5] The period for filing a protest was established as thirty days after the effective date of the law, June 15, 1927. It was thus in the obvious self-interest of the operator to demonstrate that his company had been operating a route in good faith as of January 11, 1927, since the law further required the commission to provide *new* certificates only on proof that inadequate service existed over the proposed new route.

The law was, of course, frequently misinterpreted, a condition no doubt due, at least in part, to the chaotic circumstances of the industry and the manner in which such regulations were made known in 1927. Many small operators, evidently unaware of the grandfather clause, believed that they had to go through an entirely new procedure. Others resisted and resented what they perceived as government interference. Quite a few voiced suspicions that the law was an attempt by the railroad lobby to enlist the legislature's help in putting the motorbus out of business. These wary operators predicted that the Motor Transportation Division would soon regulate the industry to the point that profits were impossible. Rumors spread that bus drivers whose route crossed a railroad passenger line would have to stop at that track and transfer passengers from the bus to the train, thus restricting buses to extremely "short haul" operations.[6]

Other operators misunderstood the terms of the grandfather clause and believed that the effective date of the law was the same as the date for establishing that they operated over a route in good faith. Rather than establishing a claim to service on or before January 11, these entrepreneurs sought to establish themselves as operators of record on June 15. In their scramble to become carriers of record, companies engaged in fare slashing and discounting. Some lines operating between Austin and San Antonio cut the fare in half, then began carrying passengers for free, and eventually began rebating up to a dollar or a free meal at the end of the line in an effort to collect passengers in support of their good faith applications.[7] Many other owners felt that the law was not valid or could not be upheld or enforced; still others "knew so little about the law that it didn't make any difference to them."[8]

The majority of operators, however, quickly learned the major features of the Beck Bus Law and attempted to comply with its provisions. Mark Marshall noted in the first report of the Motor Transportation Division that the bus operators had generally been most cooperative and helpful during the first six months of the regulatory period: "We have been gratified beyond expression at the loyal cooperation of practically all of the motor bus operators in the effort to bring about the most satisfactory results under the law, and we take this occasion to make public acknowledgement to the various motor bus operators for this co-operation."[9]

After noting the chaotic state of the industry upon inauguration of the Beck Bus Law, the first report of the Motor Transportation Division commented on compliance with insurance and safety provisions of the bill and listed the following impressive statistics:

Total Operating Revenue for Motor Bus Companies Reporting to the Commission for this period
.... $2,406,704.39
Total Operating Expenses of same for same period
.... $1,939,319.93
Total Passengers Carried......... 1,855,248
Total Schedule Miles Operated... 17,874,324.[10]

The bus business was clearly on its way to becoming a major source of travel and profit for Texans.

The Texas Bus Owners Association

Leaders in the Texas bus business quickly and shrewdly recognized the need for an organization that would represent their interests before the Legislature and the Railroad Commission. Not only was there an enormous potential profit to be nurtured and protected, but there was also the desire to comply with and interpret the provisions of the new regulatory act. An association of owners could provide news and information, lobby for favorable legislation in Austin, and generally promote investments in the bus business. Although there had been some futile efforts to organize the operators before the passage of the Beck Bus Law, it seems clear that the law itself served as the catalyst for the establishment of a viable organization.

Two key figures in the struggle to get organized were Guy J. Shields of the Southland–Red Ball Motor Bus Company and R. C. Bowen of South Texas Coaches. Their efforts to persuade others of the benefits of such an organization finally culminated in the spring of 1928, when they succeeded in forming the Texas Bus Owners Association.

Guy Shields, who was to become the first president of the Texas Bus Owners Association, spent most of his forty years in the bus business. A native of Michigan, Shields moved to Texas in 1925 as manager of the Dallas–Fort Worth Safety Coach Company after having served as president of the White Star Motor Bus Com-

A Southland–Red Ball coach (manufactured by Will) and driver in southeast Texas in the early 1930s. Motor Bus Society.

pany in Michigan and Dixie Motor Coach Lines in North Carolina. He moved from Dallas to Austin as president of the Southland Transportation Company and, when that company purchased the Red Ball Lines in 1927, became vice-president of Southland–Red Ball Motor Bus Company, operating between San Antonio and Dallas–Fort Worth. At the time of his death from a heart attack in 1930, Shields had just completed two years as president of the Texas Bus Owners Association and was assistant general manager of Southland Greyhound Lines.[11] The prominence of his position with major Texas carriers indicates the degree of support that the TBOA enjoyed in its formative period.

The second leader in the organization of the TBOA was R. C. Bowen, who served as secretary in the new association until an executive secretary could be hired

The Southland–Red Ball Motorbus Company aggressively marketed its transportation services in 1928 with ads such as this one from Texas Commercial News. Austin–Travis County Collection, Austin Public Library.

R. C. Bowen, a major figure in Texas bus history for more than three decades, had a keen sense of business and a zest for the bus industry. J. C. Carrington.

to manage its daily business. Bowen was a strong believer in regulation and, like Shields, affiliated with the nucleus of what was to become a major carrier: his lines ultimately grew into a significant portion of the National Trailways Bus System. In January, 1928, he incorporated South Texas Coaches, Inc., at Austin with a capital of $100,000. Prior to this incorporation he had been in the trucking business and had operated jitneys in the oil fields, incorporating his first line at Breckenridge in 1923.[12] At the time he helped to found the TBOA, Bowen was just beginning a long and influential career in Texas transportation, but even in 1928 he had earned high marks from his colleagues for his initiative and shrewdness.

Bowen and Shields, as well as other interested busmen, moved to incorporate the Texas Bus Owners Association on March 24, 1928. The charter of the TBOA clearly states the intention of its founders:

> The purpose for which it is formed is to form a chamber of commerce and board of trade with power to provide and maintain rooms for the conduct of their business and to establish and maintain uniformity in the commercial usages of cities and towns insofar as they pertain to the operation of motor bus transportation; to acquire, preserve, and disseminate valuable business information and to adopt rules and regulations which shall govern all transactions connected with such business and generally to promote the interest of the bus business and increase the facilities for the accommodation of the public.[13]

The eleven directors signing the document were R. C. Bowen, Fort Worth; W. E. Nunnelee, Tyler; Howard Parks, Dallas; C. M. Hannan, Paris; H. L. Burt, Gonzales; Sam Day, Waco; Fred Freeman, Denton; J. J. Thompson, Breckenridge; W. S. White, Dallas; Joe Amberson, San Antonio; and Guy J. Shields, Austin. The charter was notarized and filed in the office of Secretary of State James Y. McCallum on March 26, and the new organization was given tax-exempt status at that time.[14]

President Shields called the first meeting of the association almost immediately, and the Board of Directors convened for the first time at 8:15 P.M. on April 4, 1928, at the Jefferson Hotel in Dallas. The group of ten (W. E. Nunnelee missed this meeting) quickly approved the new charter and elected Guy J. Shields president, Fred Freeman vice-president, and R. C. Bowen treasurer.[15]

Although Shields had appointed Bowen to act as secretary for the meeting, it seemed apparent to the group that a permanent secretary-manager should be appointed to conduct the business of the association. The minutes reflect that the members thought this issue important enough to require that all candidates for this position personally appear before the board. Thompson moved and White seconded that the annual salary for a secretary-manager not exceed thirty-six hundred dollars, "until such times as our Treasury would permit an increase."[16] Freeman then moved and Burt seconded that another meeting be called in Austin on April 13, "for the purpose of engaging our Secretary-Manager." Since the Railroad Commission was planning to meet in Austin on April 14 to formally adopt and announce additional motorbus regulations, Hannan and Amberson offered a motion to convene a general meeting at 8:00 P.M. on the thirteenth, also in Austin, to solicit general membership and to go over the rules of the RCT with the operators attending the meeting. Before adjournment at 12:15 A.M. on April 5, President Shields had organized five committees, the names of which clearly indicate the topics of importance to the new organization:

Legislative and Legal................. R. C. Bowen
Finance and Auditing..................... H. L. Burt
Membership........................Sam H. Day
Information, Advertising, and
Publicity......................... Howard Parks
Equipment, Operating and
Good Roads...................Charles Hannan.[17]

The second meeting of the Board of Directors of the TBOA convened at the Driskill Hotel in Austin at 2:15 P.M. on April 13, 1928. The minutes contain several references to the hectic conditions under which the directors were meeting, since the city was crowded with bus operators gathering to hear the forthcoming decisions of the Railroad Commission. Thus Howard Parks and Will White arrived four hours late, the members directed Bowen's Legislative and Legal Committee "to take such action as they deem necessary in any case of emergency" dealing with the RCT, and ultimately the meeting adjourned and reconvened at the Stephen F. Austin Hotel at 8:00 the next morning to conclude business before adjourning to attend the commission sessions. The directors then reconvened in a hearing room in the commission chambers just before the lunch hour on the fourteenth.[18]

Despite the evident confusion, on April 13, 1928, the group did in fact interview six candidates for the position of secretary-manager: "Mr. J. C. Carrington, Jack

Utecht, Colonel Stockton, Judge Nelson, J. C. Duvall, and Judge Gamble." On the morning of the fourteenth, "after a long discussion regarding several candidates for the Secretary-Manager position, the election followed. Motion made by Nunnelee and seconded by Hannan. That, J. C. Carrington be unanimously elected. Carried."[19]

The official letter of Carrington's appointment is dated April 20, 1928. President Shields indicates the need for the new secretary-manager "to let matters stand as they are and come to Austin to represent us on May 1st." The letter stipulates the salary to be three hundred dollars per month, the maximum salary figure agreed to by the initial meeting of the board.[20] At the time of the letter Carrington was executive secretary of the Chamber of Commerce in Cuero and had had little direct experience with the motor coach industry. He was soon to become, however, one of the most influential figures in the history of Texas bus lines.

The same meetings of the Board of Directors that resulted in Carrington's appointment focused, of course, on the forthcoming operating regulations to be issued on the fourteenth by the Railroad Commission. The set of forty-five rules ultimately released served to amplify and clarify the Beck Bus Law. The rules primarily concerned safety and stipulated that drivers should be at least eighteen years of age and free of physical and mental deficiencies that might inhibit proper operation of the bus. Additional regulations prohibited the use of intoxicants, specified conditions of baggage handling and other carrier responsibilities, and required operators to adhere to a reasonably regular schedule and to file all changes of tariff and schedule through the Motor Transportation Division. Rule 35 further stipulated that any interruption in service "of more than twenty-four hours duration" be reported promptly to the commission along with an explanation of the cause of the delay.[21] These rules were to be put into effect as of June 1, 1928, and seemed to meet with the approval of most bus owners. At its third meeting, on May 25 at the Hotel Texas in Fort Worth, the TBOA Board unanimously endorsed the regulations as the first order of business.[22]

The minutes of this third meeting bear scrutiny, since they reveal an organization moving from the initial phase

SOUTHLAND-RED BALL MOTORBUS CO.

207 WEST 4TH ST.
PHONE 2-3266

AUSTIN, TEXAS

April 20, 1928

Mr. J. C. Carrington,
Chamber of Commerce,
Cuero, Texas.

Dear Mr. Carrington:

    The writer takes great pleasure in notifying you, of your appointment to the office of Secretary-Manager of The Texas Bus Owners Association. The salary is to be three hundred dollars ($300.00) per month.

    Mr. Burt has informed me that you have already made the necessary arrangements for a two months leave of absence from your present connection, effective May 1st. It might be a very good idea for you to let matters stand as they are and come to Austin to represent us on May 1st, then in case our organization should not develope as expected you would still have this other opportunity.

    Of course the above is just a friendly suggestion and take it for what it is worth as I feel that if we all get behind the new Association as we should it is bound to be a great success.

    With best regards to you and hoping to see you soon in Austin, I am,

Very truly yours

TEXAS BUS OWNERS ASS'N, INC.,

Guy J. Shields
Pres.

GJS/J

By this letter, Guy Shields, president of the Texas Bus Owners Association, hired the man who was to become the only secretary-manager the association ever had—Joe C. Carrington. J. C. Carrington.

of assemblage and self-generation into the next phase, in which the agenda items become more specific and the continuance of the organization becomes a presumption. By the May 25 meeting, J. C. Carrington had replaced R. C. Bowen as the keeper of the minutes and had begun to assume other important duties. The minutes now begin to reflect a common pattern: reports of liaison with the Railroad Commission and other state agencies; committee reports on matters of current interest to the association; acceptance of applications for new membership; inquiries by oil, tire, and equipment companies interested in contractual arrangements with the TBOA and its members; and the escalating degree to which all of these matters become delegated to the secretary-manager. Specific concerns of the May 25 meeting included the continuing effort to publish a statewide guide that would incorporate all known schedules of TBOA members and the report from "Mr. Townsend of Stone and Webster" that the next session of the legislature would see the introduction of bills designed to increase the tax burden of the operators.[23]

For the May 25 meeting Secretary Carrington had prepared a "Suggested Plan of Work," which the members of the board "took home for further study" and which became de facto the agenda of the TBOA for the rest of its existence. Carrington divided his program into five components: public relations, publicity, standardization, operating matters, and legislative and legal matters. Under the fifth category he proposed four goals:

  a. Keep the Legislators properly informed about the activities of bus operation
  b. Cooperate with the Railroad and Highway Commission
  c. Oppose any attempted legislation that is harmful to the bus owners
  d. Secure such favorable legislation as can [be secured] for the benefit of the bus owners.[24]

In addition to these legislative and legal matters, the program of work addressed, under the two headings of Public Relations and Publicity, a major implicit concern of the directors: that the traveling public be made increasingly aware of the advantages of bus travel. Given the

Inside the Southland garage about 1930 workers prepare a "Greyhound of the Highways" for passenger service. The bus is composed of a wooden frame covered by very thin sheet metal. It has a distended gas cap and rear emergency door. Motor Bus Society.

condition of many of the roads, a public fear that needed to be overcome quickly was the widespread opinion that perhaps the motor buses were not safe. Much of the public relations effort of TBOA over the years was devoted to promoting the safety records of the operators. Items such as the uniform publication of schedules, the acquisition of appropriate insurance, the use of quality equipment from suppliers such as the Texas Company and Gulf Oil, and the RCT regulations forbidding drivers to use narcotics or intoxicants were all given maximum publicity by the TBOA through Carrington's untiring efforts. In the same vein at the meeting of May 25, Sam Day moved and H. L. Burt seconded the motion that the secretary prepare a Code of Ethics for consideration by the directors at a future meeting.[25] The object of the code was to demonstrate to the public that the bus owners were reliable businessmen who had the interests of the traveler at heart.

Carrington lost no time devising a statement, and the fifth meeting of the TBOA directors formally endorsed the Code of Ethics while meeting in Dallas on July 25, 1928. Using the Golden Rule as its stated premise, the code addresses itself to three audiences on behalf of the TBOA owner/member: the general public, other bus operators, and the owner/member himself. Although the document provides no specified sanctions, it implies that all operators will do their best to live up to their obligations toward all three of the addressed constituencies. Its tone is best illustrated in the first article, under the heading "To the General Public": "The bus owner should consider himself a public servant and his every act should be performed with that thought in mind."[26] The code was widely disseminated and sent to all members along with copies appropriate for posting in offices and terminals, and it formed the cover for the third issue (October, 1928) of the association's new journal, *Motor Transportation in Texas*.

In one regard the Code of Ethics deviates somewhat from its very general language: the eleventh article takes a stand against what the directors regarded as the unethical practice of operating below cost:

> The bus owner should not depart from good business principles. The expense of doing business, such as wear and tear on equipment, interest on money invested, rents, taxes, insurance, and all other items of expense should be ever before his eyes. Never, under any circumstances, should the minimum cost, plus a fair profit, be departed from. He should feel here a double restraint: in the first place, to establish rates or make contracts for less than cost of operation will limit his service to the public and depreciate the service rendered; in the second place, it is wrong.[27]

The directness of language in this eleventh article illustrates a persistent problem that the organization still faced in mid-1928 with wildcatters and operators who would slash prices illegally to force the competition out of business. A specific instance was reported to the directors at the May 25 meeting:

Mr. Day reported an instance in Waco where one Mr. Nat Hays, who is a school teacher there and at certain times of the year operates a number of small trucks hauling passengers without a permit, etc. He stated that he felt confident that the same practice was going on in other parts of the state and thought the Association should take some action in curbing the violators. Motion made by Parks, seconded by Day, that the Association take such action necessary to protect its members against these illegal operators.[28]

Again the secretary-manager acted, and before the end of the year the adjutant general and the attorney general instructed their agencies to go after the wildcatters. Adjutant General Robert L. Robertson issued a memorandum "to Texas Rangers and Other Peace Officers of the State" on December 14, urging diligence in the prosecution of those not in compliance with the Beck Bus Law: "There are a number of persons known as 'wild-catters' now operating motor busses for hire over the public highways of this state without complying with the law or procuring a permit from the Railroad Commission. Therefore, I now respectively [sic] request that you give your hearty cooperation to the enforcement of the penal provisions of the motor bus statute passed by the last Legislature."

On the same date, and evidently acting on the same request from Carrington's office, Attorney General Claude Pollard distributed a letter to all county attorneys in Texas directing their attention, in language similar to Robertson's, toward the penal provisions of the Beck Bus Law and concluding: "Certainly, the legitimate bus operators who have complied with the law in every particular, and who are strictly observing the rules and regulations of the Railroad Commission, are now entitled to the protection which the law contemplates that they should receive."

Through such efforts the TBOA continued to establish itself as the central organization of operators in the state, and gradually the problem of illegal carriers began to come under control. As late as the 1930s, however, wildcatting remained a problem. Those who owned autos during the Depression were often tempted to use them to generate extra income. Thus on August 13, 1930, Ranger C. D. Hawkins apprehended one Charlie Williamson of Dallas, who had advertised in the Fort Worth newspapers to take persons on trips if part of the expenses were defrayed. Williamson was charged with having no identification plates, no motor coach permit, and no license.[29]

As a further means of solidifying the new organization, Secretary-Manager Carrington decided to produce a newsletter, which would keep members informed of the work of the association. This undertaking began almost as soon as Carrington arrived in Austin and was at first a mimeographed sheet distributed as *Bus Chatter*. Arrangements were quickly made for a more permanent sort of journal, however, and the first issue of the TBOA house organ, *Motor Transportation in Texas*, appeared in August 1928. "Bus Chatter" continued as a popular news and notes feature of the new periodical.[30] Carrington served as the initial editor of the journal, although staff members soon were added to handle the burgeoning press of duties centralizing in the Austin office. By 1930 Wendell O'Neal had joined the staff as editor of *Motor Transportation*, F. N. Clifford held the title of membership secretary, and H. S. Glisson had become assistant manager in charge of bus guides and schedules.[31] Carrington had almost at once secured the inestimable services of Gladys McCarty as secretary to the secretary-manager, and to her fell many of the duties involving liaison with the Motor Transportation Division, as well as correspondence with the bus owners themselves.[32]

As 1928 drew to a close, the TBOA had every reason to be proud of its initial successes. In its first few months, it had survived the initial phase of organization, defined its goals, hired an effective executive secretary, produced a code of ethics, acted on major legislative developments, secured the assistance of the State of Texas in disrupting wildcat operations, begun a journal, and generally established itself as the collective representative of the intercity bus lines. Carrington, Shields, Bowen, and the others no doubt concluded 1928 with a genuine sense of accomplishment as they planned for the first annual convention of the Texas Bus Owners Association to be held at the Adolphus Hotel in Dallas on April 15–16, 1929.

Relations with the Railroad Commission and Others

Cooperation between the Texas Bus Owners Association and the Railroad Commission of Texas continued throughout this formative period. Not only had the bus owners generally encouraged the establishment of the Motor Transportation Division under the Beck Bus Law, but they also had applauded the vast majority of the decisions of the Railroad Commission. The Motor Transportation Division again publicly congratulated the owners in its report to the governor at the close of 1928:

> What they have lacked, however, in knowledge and training in transportation matters, they have made up by a fine spirit of co-operation with this Commission in working out the common problems which have confronted them and the Commission in putting into effect the Motor Bus Law. The instances where we have not had the wholehearted co-operation of those engaged in the industry have been very rare, and we wish to make acknowledgement for this effort to join the Commission in its difficult and delicate task of administering this new law.[33]

The commission report then continued to divulge the statistics for the Texas bus industry in 1928: 4,744,867 passengers carried without a single fatality or serious injury; 969 buses operated by 222 individuals and corporations; 45,982,435 bus miles operated over a 31,000-mile bus route network. Total operating revenue amounted to $6,412,483.50 for calendar year 1928, while total operating expenses were $5,717,668.17.[34] Even when one considers that the comparable report for 1927 covered only the last six calendar months of operations, these impressive statistics demonstrate that the bus industry in Texas was continuing to prosper.

Three other events in the autumn of 1928 warranted special attention from the bus operators. Representatives of the public utilities commissions of Colorado, New Mexico, Oklahoma, and Louisiana met with RCT representatives in Amarillo on September 6 to discuss possible interstate regulation of the carriers. In October the Railroad Commission granted the first intrastate permit to an interstate bus line, allowing Texas-Oklahoma Coaches the authority to operate between Dallas and Henrietta. In November a subsidiary of the Cotton Belt Railway, Southwestern Transportation Company, acquired the extensive operations of the W. E. Nunnelee Bus Line, headquartered in Tyler, for a reported $250,000.[35]

The mutual respect of the Motor Transportation Division and the Texas Bus Owners Association continued in 1929. In his first annual report as secretary-manager for TBOA, J. C. Carrington wrote: "At this time we must not forget the cooperation rendered by Hon. Mark Marshall and the members of the Railroad Commission. While the operators might not be satisfied with every decision that they have rendered, yet no one will deny that they have been just and equitable in the administration of these affairs."[36]

Indeed, during March of 1929 the TBOA went to the trouble of sponsoring a "Good Will and Education Tour," which involved nine district meetings in various parts of the state. These meetings attracted over three hundred bus operators, according to Carrington and O'Neal, and were held in Houston, Nacogdoches, Dallas, Fort Worth, Wichita Falls, Amarillo, Lubbock, Sweetwater, and San Angelo.[37] The presence of Mark Marshall on this tour, along with State Rep. J. C. Duvall, illustrates the rapport between the TBOA and the state regulatory agencies.

The culmination of the tour came in San Antonio, two days after the last district meeting in San Angelo, with the grand opening of the new San Antonio terminal on March 28, 1929. Clarence E. Gilmore, chairman of the RCT, delivered a radio address in conjunction with the opening ceremonies. Gilmore's themes were the same as those of Carrington and Marshall: the motor bus industry is booming, its safety record is unimpeachable, and its leaders cooperate with the regulatory agencies: "With the rarest exception, the Railroad Commission has had the fullest and most complete co-operation of the owners and operators of motor busses in the development and perfection of a plan for their operation with the view to serving in the fullest and highest degree the convenience and necessity of the public."[38]

The spirit of cooperation continued throughout 1929.

Built at a cost of $350,000, the new San Antonio terminal opened officially on March 28, 1929, and epitomized the very latest in bus station facilities. The Southland–Red Ball bus in this view is turning north onto East Martin Street off Navarro. Motor Bus Society.

In August the TBOA provided the bus for the transportation of RCT officials to the convention of the National Association of Railroad and Public Utility Commissioners held at Glacier National Park. J. C. Carrington accompanied the state officials.

Chairman Gilmore died unexpectedly, however, on October 10, 1929, in San Antonio. Governor Moody replaced him with former governor Pat Neff, who became the chairman of the Railroad Commission in January of 1930, serving with fellow commissioners Lon Smith and C. V. Terrell. Under Neff's leadership the commission settled into the task, begun under Gilmore, of processing the large number of applications before it. During this busy period the RCT, acting on the recommendations of its Motor Transportation Division, had the duty not only of issuing permits and certificates but also of presiding

Passengers, porters, and the curious watch the operations as baggage handlers load Southland–Red Ball #135 at the San Antonio terminal's main bus drive. Motor Bus Society.

over such "housekeeping" details as terminal relocation, the setting of fares and the establishment of schedules, applications for schedule changes, and the approval of detours and temporary routings.

The Forty-first Legislature approved the appointment of four inspectors for the Motor Transportation Division because vehicle safety was yet another concern of the Railroad Commission. The four initial inspectors selected were John Alderman of Fort Worth; J. H. Edwards of Merkel; Sam Johnson of Johnson City, the father of the future president of the United States; and O. E. Walters of Sulphur Springs.[39] J. C. Carrington remembered Sam Johnson, in his capacity as an inspector, as one who "took the job seriously and was always a pleasant man to have around—a good man to work with."[40]

Carrington himself remained quite busy throughout this formative period, establishing good working relations not only with the inspectors and the members of the regulatory agencies but also with the operators. One of his main responsibilities was the planning of the TBOA

Making a bus trip a social occasion, a group of prominent San Antonians prepares to leave by motor coach: J. A. Knutson, Paul Tibbetts, W. E. Pine, Mrs. Alex Adams, and Mrs. E. L. Austin at the San Antonio terminal, about 1929. The San Antonio Light Collection, the University of Texas Institute of Texan Cultures at San Antonio.

conventions, the first of which occurred on April 15–16, 1929, at the Adolphus Hotel in Dallas. According to Carrington's report in *Motor Transportation in Texas*, more than two hundred attended. The agenda was very crowded, and serious business occupied a large part of the delegates' time. The morning session featured State Rep. Walter Beck of Fort Worth, who had authored the original Motor Bus Law, with a rather lengthy speech covering such matters as the gasoline tax, forthcoming legislation concerning license plate fees, and gaps in the existing state highway system.[41]

C. V. Terrell's afternoon address to the convention emphasized the cooperation between the TBOA and the Railroad Commission. Commissioner Terrell praised the operators "for their success in lifting the bus industry from the hack and jitney stage to its present status" and went on to note that not a single passenger had been killed or seriously injured of the "ten million passengers" carried since the Beck Bus Law went into effect. Other speakers at the convention included State Rep.

The Texas Bus Owners Association provided the transportation when state officials attended the National Convention of Railroad and Public Utility Commissioners at Glacier National Park in the summer of 1929. Mark Marshall, director of the Railroad Commission's Motor Transportation Division, is second man from the left in the front row. J. C. Carrington is at the far right. J. C. Carrington.

J. C. Duvall and George Short, the former attorney general of Oklahoma, who discussed the efforts at interstate regulation being made by the states in the absence of federal regulations regarding the bus industry.[42]

By the time of the second annual convention of the TBOA, in San Antonio on April 8–10, 1930, Carrington had become even busier. He had become acting secretary of the Texas Truck Owners Association and was engaged in working for legislation favorable to both truck and bus operators. He had overseen the considerable expansion of his office staff and had become deeply involved with H. S. Glisson in the production and promotion of the bus guide known as the "Texas Traveler's Guide," which ultimately became the *Official National Bus Guide* or "Green Guide" familiar to agents and operators throughout the Southwest. *Motor Transportation in Texas* has expanded to a three-state clientele and was moving beyond Texas, Oklahoma, and Arkansas so quickly that its name had been changed to *Motor Transportation* in early 1930 to reflect its wider appeal. In May of 1930 Carrington was elected secretary-treasurer of the newly formed General Traffic Association of the Motor Coach Operators of North America. Despite these additional duties, however, he continued in his leadership of the TBOA.

Because his days with the Cuero Chamber of Commerce had taught him the value of public relations in business dealings, Carrington continued to work through the various chambers in his efforts to develop both clientele and favorable regulations for the bus operators. Typical of his procedure was a circular letter sent to all Chamber of Commerce secretaries in Texas on June 2, 1930, in which he solicited interest on behalf of the Texas Commercial Executives Association for a workshop to be held later that month in Plainview. While touting the advantages of the workshop for chamber secretaries and exhorting them to learn how to get the most value for each chamber dollar expended, Carrington also promoted the bus industry: "A. T. Barrett, President of this Association, and myself will not have the privilege of being with you at this school because we are busy trying to work out a program for you whereby your town can be more economically served and more service can be given you by the motor bus companies."[43] He enclosed a current copy of the "Texas Traveler's Guide" for each chamber official.

The response to such circular letters was generally quite strong. After a typical mailing on April 19, 1929, asking for reactions to the bus service from the chamber secretaries, he received positive replies from such diverse communities as Madisonville and Shamrock, Pampa and San Benito, Dallas and Fort Stockton.[44] A few of these letters bear examination because they reflect the importance of the bus industry to the local communities and thus to the commerce of Texas as a whole.

J. E. Guthrie of Salado, signing himself as "Druggist" and "Secretary, Chamber of Commerce," replied to Carrington on May 17, 1929, in a handwritten note: "Years ago Salado being an inland town felt great need of a Rail Road. We no longer need one. We have 6 Greyhound Busses each way in 24 hours. Our people like the Service—the bus line fills a long felt want."

One of the strongest endorsements of the bus industry came from Ed C. Burris, secretary of the Jasper Chamber of Commerce, on May 3, 1929. Burris, writing on letterhead advertising "Jasper County—The New Land of Canaan," extolled the virtues of bus transportation by stating that "it is not possible for an individual or group of individuals to estimate the importance of Bus transportation in Texas and the United States." He continued:

> You take this town for an example and I feel that there are numerous other communities in which similar conditions exist. We can depend upon the Bus service for more frequent means of getting about than the Railroad. This condition is not brought about by neglect of the Railroad but is made possible by six Highways radiating out of our little town. Each of these Highways accommodate from one to three Buses each way every day, . . . The Buses assist the surrounding communities in reaching our little city for shopping and other business purposes. This manner of service could not be rendered by any other means of transportation.

An equally enthusiastic reply, dated April 23, 1929, came from O. L. Talley, secretary of the Stephenville Chamber of Commerce: "We are very much pleased to inform you that the Roberson Bus Lines, who are serving this community, are rendering excellent service; we could not do without them. We do not hesitate to say that the motorbus is a great asset to Stephenville and its trade territory. It is filling an important part in the development of the agricultural and industrial progress of this section of the State."

Through these endorsements and other similar projects, Carrington kept the name of the Texas Bus Owners Association constantly before the public, the regulatory agencies, and the operators. Other aspects of his public relations efforts included contacts with the local news outlets and such promotional efforts as the Motor Bus Clergy Certificates. The office in the Littlefield Building increased its activity with the addition of both the Texas Truck Owners Association and the National Motor Bus Clergy Bureau. Through the latter, Carrington offered reduced rates to clergy and acted as a clearinghouse for requests from ministers for reduced fares. He began the service late in 1929 and had enrolled thousands of clergy by 1932. In his appeals to the bus operators to support such a bureau, Carrington argued that giving clergy a small reduction in fare (typically 10 percent) would reap benefits for the operators because the clergy were influential community leaders who could persuade their congregations and other community members of the virtues of bus travel. He also pointed out that the railroads uniformly provided such a service, and that clergy had a right to expect similar reductions from the bus lines.[45]

The Texas Motor Transportation Association

By the time of the third annual convention of the TBOA, the Great Depression was in full force and the bus lines of Texas were entering a period of consolidation and merger. The issues facing the industry were becoming more similar to those confronting the trucking industry, and despite Carrington's pledge to the TBOA in 1930 that no effort would ever be made to consolidate the TBOA and the TTOA (Texas Truck Owners Association), the convention agenda must have raised doubts about that pledge—and, indeed, about the wisdom of keeping the interests of the two organizations separate. Both truckers and busmen were evidently destined to fight a common enemy: the railroads. State Rep. Walter H. Beck

In this August, 1929, view of Missouri Pacific motor coach #569, the awnings, observation lights, rounded rear windows, observation platform, and drumhead light clearly reflect the influence of railroad observation car design. Motor Bus Society.

again addressed the bus operators on the first day of their convention, June 15, 1931, at the Hotel Texas in Fort Worth. Beck went straight to his main point:

> The entire complexion of highway legislation in Texas has changed completely in the last few months. Regulation was originally intended to insure economical, efficient regulation for the public benefit; the passage of HB 336 makes the principle one of forcing the trucks to operate under conditions that will force them out of existence. From that it is only a step to forcing the busses out. The interests in bus lines owned by the railroads are so insignificant comparatively speaking that they would gladly sacrifice them to get rid of the busses.[46]

The legislation Beck referred to was quite complex but essentially imposed stringent conditions on truck operations, principally in the area of insurance. The perpetrator, of course, was the railroad industry, at least in the view of the bus and truck operators. The new laws also included severe weight restrictions, which the truckers thought reduced their ability to compete effectively with the railroads, and enhanced requirements for obtaining permits and operating licenses.[47]

But it was the insurance aspect of the new regulations that most frustrated the truckers and busmen. Carrington, ever alert to the changing needs of the operators, accordingly formed, capitalized, and underwrote a new organization called Motor Carrier Insurance Agency (MCIA) and brought the new company into existence with a lead article in *Motor Transportation* in August of 1931. The new business had its headquarters in the Littlefield Building in Austin. At the time of its inception, the Motor Carrier Insurance Agency shared its guiding spirit, Joe C. Carrington, with the other organizations of which he was also the chief of daily operations: Texas Bus Owners Association, Texas Truck Owners Service Bureau, General Traffic Association of Motor Bus Operators of North America, Motor Bus Clergy Bureau, National Clergy Bureau, *Official Bus Guides*, and *Motor Transportation*. A. T. Barrett was designated as "Head" of the MCIA, however, and six field representatives were hired across the state and distributed at Brady, Houston, Tyler, Paris, Fort Worth, and Amarillo. Further credibility for the new agency came from the enlistment of Bryan Bell as handler of the technical operations of the company. Bell had formerly been with the Motor Transportation Division of the RCT and was the specialist in bus insurance; William Ford of San Antonio, well known in trucking, took over the truck insurance segment of the business.[48]

In areas other than insurance, the growing amalgamation of the TBOA and the TTOA continued to have an impact on the rights of their constituencies. HB 628, for example, had been another source of irritation to the truckers because of its severe limitations on the approved weight that a trucker engaged in the hauling of cotton or cotton products could legally transport. With the support of the TTOA and TBOA, a temporary injunction was awarded to the J. H. McLeaish Trucking Company, a cotton-hauling firm, in federal court in Houston on August 1, 1931. According to an enthusiastic report in *Motor Transportation*, "In a rather lengthy statement, the court pointed out that the provisions of the act were calculated to be an oppression upon a particular class rather than strictly a protective measure for the highways."[49]

As a result of the desire to fight the common enemy (felt to be the railroads), the need for economic efficiency of operation during the difficult years of the Great Depression, and a dawning realization about their many common interests and objectives, the truck and bus owners continued to draw closer together. In early 1932 the metamorphosis into yet another organization took place with the emergence of the Texas Motor Transportation Association (TMTA). By July of 1932 the new association was in full control of the public relations, lobbying, contractual arrangements, convention planning, and general codification of the rules governing the bus and truck operators of the state.

Officers of the Texas Motor Transportation Association included Tom Jones, Dallas, president; Walter H. Beck (still a member of the Texas legislature), Fort Worth, executive vice-president and general manager; and J. C. Carrington, Austin, secretary. None of the state directors of the new association were primarily bus operators.[50]

According to *Motor Transportation*, the TMTA would have five categories of membership: private owners and shippers who depended on highway transportation; for-hire truck operators; bus operators of all kinds; the trade, including bus and truck manufacturers, service stations, concrete firms, and the like; and "dollar members," a phrase used to denote employees of members, friends of highway transportation, and truck salesmen.[51] The emphasis was clearly away from the single-constituency focus of the TBOA and on legislation and public relations programs favorable to highway users in general. A survey of the articles and even the covers of various issues of *Motor Transportation* quickly reflects this trend: in September of 1932, *Motor Transportation* contains not a single article devoted primarily to bus line concerns. Virtually all of the articles from mid-1932 on deal with questions of legislation, vehicle maintenance, or enhanced efficiency. Most of the articles concern themselves with a nationally developing audience, and Texas concerns are relegated to a feature section. "Bus Chatter" had totally disappeared from the journal by late 1932. Although Carrington and others ultimately organized a "Bus Division" of the TMTA, it was clear by mid-1932 that the primary focus of TMTA efforts would not be on the bus lines.

A corollary to the decline of bus influence within the Texas organization, however, was the continued development of national organizations to serve the interests of bus operators coast to coast. Many Texas operators were turning their attention to interstate routes, and the expansion of bus lines (covered in chapters three and four) caused Texas to become less insulated from the rest of the nation's bus operations. The National Association of Motor Bus Owners had begun in the mid-twenties, and Carrington attended its annual convention, along with other Texans, at Atlantic City, New Jersey, on September 28–29, 1931. Also attending from Texas were Paul W. Tibbetts, president of Southland Greyhound Lines; C. B. DeBerry, General Traffic Manager of Southwestern Transportation Company; and John H. Awtry, General Counsel of Sunshine Bus Lines. A. W. Riter of Sunshine Bus Lines and Dixie Motor Coach Lines was elected regional director to replace TBOA's A. T. Barrett, who had recently retired from the bus business.[52] *Bus Transportation*, a national journal functioning as the house organ for the National Association of Motor Bus Owners (NAMBO) subsumed much of the material once covered in *Motor Transportation in Texas*.

Carrington delivered what turned out to be a "final" report on the Texas Bus Owners Association on September 1, 1931, in a document stressing the accomplishments of the organization.[53] At the time of the report he had affiliated the TBOA with NAMBO, the National Safety Council, the United States Good Roads Association, the United States Chamber of Commerce, the Texas Trade Executives Association, the Texas Commercial Executives Association, and the Austin Chamber of Com-

This parlor observation coach, "Miss Texas," saw limited service with Texas Bus Lines between Houston and Galveston around 1930. This photograph is evidence that the SceniCruisers and VistaLiners of the 1950s were not the first double-decker intercity coaches on Texas highways. Tom Amick.

merce. Eighty-five bus companies and their affiliates held membership in the TBOA, which represented virtually every bus operator in the state of Texas.[54]

Indeed, if the TBOA did seem to pass out of corporate existence as it amalgamated its interests with those of the truckers and the shippers, it had at least served its purpose. Organization and regulation had come to Texas rather smoothly under the leadership of men like Mark Marshall, R. C. Bowen, Pat Neff, Guy Shields, Clarence Gilmore, Walter H. Beck, J. C. Duvall, Sam Day, Lon Smith, C. V. Terrell, A. T. Barrett, and, of course, Joe Carrington. The primary story from 1927 to 1931–32 had been the efforts to organize. The next story would be the efforts to merge, to stabilize, and to survive the Great Depression.

3. The Depression and the Coming of the War

Until the advent of regulation in 1927, the story of the Texas intercity bus industry had been the story of individual pioneers: L. H. Creamer, Ed Abbott, O. C. Murphey, Walter Painter, W. B. Chenoweth, Josh Merritt, and dozens of others had ventured into the business from other enterprises. Many succeeded and, of course, many others failed, in establishing viable schedules and profitable operations. Survivors such as Sam Day, R. C. Bowen, G. W. Hyde, and others remained active in the business for many years, while many such as W. E. Nunnelee and Fred Freeman sold out their bus interests and turned to other pursuits.[1]

With regulation came increased complexity. It was no longer legal for a person to purchase or borrow an old touring car, advertise in the local newspaper for passengers, collect the fares, and head off down the road. J. C. Carrington and the Texas Bus Owners Association had come down hard on these wildcatters and in a variety of measures had successfully brought the bus operators in Texas under the organizational umbrella of TBOA. With their general interests protected by the TBOA and the Railroad Commission, the legitimate operators now turned their attention to consolidation of route structures and the development of additional traffic and revenue.

A rather natural avenue for enhanced traffic seemed to lie in expanded route systems, which would enable passengers and freight to travel longer distances without changing coaches or lines. This through service would presumably benefit both passenger and operator: the traveler would not be inconvenienced by frequent changes and terminal layovers, and the operator would develop additional revenues by being able to originate passengers from more communities.

Greyhound and others explored the possibilities of air-to-bus transfers at an early stage of commercial aviation history. A. T. Barrett's brother, A. P., appeared at the Fort Worth TBOA convention of 1931 to promote the concept. The location of this airstrip has not been identified. Motor Bus Society.

By the end of the 1920s, therefore, Texas bus operators were consolidating their through routes and engaging in mergers that would strengthen their competitive positions against each other and against the railroads. "Bus Chatter" even reported airline connections as early as 1929: "The Western Air Express and the Pickwick Greyhound Motor Coach Lines have linked in a transcontinental bus-air service. The airline operates between Kansas City and Los Angeles. The Pickwick busses run from Los Angeles through El Paso, Oklahoma City, Kansas City, St. Louis and the East. A bus, for example, will take Oklahoma City passengers to Amarillo where they will board a plane for Los Angeles."[2] Earlier in that same year Texas Air Transport began bus-air connections at Love Field in Dallas with the intention of operating through service that would connect small towns to those with airport facilities.[3]

Despite the interest that these early air-bus connections might have for historians, the major intercity bus effort on the eve of the thirties in Texas was directed at extending highway route structures through merger and franchise acquisition. In March of 1929, A. P. Barrett, owner of the Dixie Coach Corporation, announced purchases of lines in North Texas that resulted in Dixie Motor Coaches, an amalgamation of routes that covered 1,023 miles and encompassed a five-million-dollar operation: "Ninety-three buses are in constant use with eight in reserve, and the company owns eight of the thirteen union terminals along its route. The total personnel of the company now numbers 190 persons, of whom 105 are drivers, 23 mechanics, and 37 terminal employees."[4]

Other mergers and consolidations surrounded the territory of Dixie Motor Coaches. The Missouri Pacific Railroad had formed a highway transportation subsidiary in September of 1928, and by February of 1929 was operating 125 buses over eighteen hundred route miles in Missouri, Texas, and Arkansas. Like the Cotton Belt, the Santa Fe, and other large railroads, the Missouri Pacific wanted to stem the tide of bus competition, which had helped depress railroad passenger revenues during the twenties. The railroads would typically form highway subsidiaries by purchasing small competing bus routes, but rather than shutting down these routes, they would operate buses in complementary service to the passenger trains. On many routes the operation of a bus was all that the traffic seemed to require, and the railroad could realize a considerable saving in overhead.[5]

The most impressive of these route mergers prior to the 1930s, however, occurred in the fall of 1929, when R. C. Bowen sold his interest in three bus lines to what was then still known as the Southland–Red Ball Motor Bus Company. The new organization thus began life as Southland Greyhound Lines just before the stock market crash in 1929. Bowen received a reported $1,150,000 for West Texas Coaches, South Texas Coaches, and Young's Bus Line.[6] *Motor Transportation in Texas* reported the statistics in a lead story headlined, "Huge Merger Effected": "Included in this network are most of the leading cities of the state, the majority of the college centers, and industrial headquarters of practically every part of Texas. Total mileage of the operations is 2000 miles, exclusive of options. Equipment totals 200 coaches ranging from seven to 34-passenger capacity. Replacement of the present equipment at a cost of $1,000,000, however, will begin immediately." Officers

Studebaker touring buses of the Missouri Pacific Transportation Company are deep in the Rio Grande Valley at McAllen during a springtime excursion in 1931. Motor Bus Society.

of the new corporation included E. C. Eckstrom, president and general manager; Guy J. Shields, assistant general manager; and M. S. Wren, traffic manager. R. C. Bowen was to "assist officials in the operations of the lines until reorganization is completed."[7]

The merger was something of a coup for Bowen, who had worked hard to put it together and who was destined to receive his cash settlement about one week prior to the crash. The Railroad Commission actually approved the merger in hearings conducted in Austin on September 17, 1929, although Commissioners Gilmore, Terrell, and Smith made their order effective two weeks later, on October 1. The hearing followed a rather typical format: notices were duly posted, the purchasing company was investigated, its intent was discovered, and the public was invited to the hearing:

> Although ten days notice of the time and place of the hearing had been given to the applicants, to all interested parties and to the public generally, no protests were prosecuted against the proposed sale and transfer of said certificates, and it appearing to the Commission, after carefully considering the evidence introduced at the hearing that the application for the Commission's approval of the sale and transfer was made in good faith by

both the purchaser and the seller; that the Southland Red–Ball Motorbus Company is acquiring the new certificates for the purpose of operating motor busses over the routes and not for the purpose of speculating upon them; that the proposed purchaser is financially able and in every other way qualified to operate the service in a dependable and satisfactory manner, and that the proposed purchaser is willing, ready and able to operate such service in compliance with the law and in accordance with the rules and regulations prescribed, or which may hereafter be prescribed by the Railroad Commission of Texas, the sale and transfer is approved.[8]

Similar action on the same date transferred the certificates of Young's Bus Line, R. C. Bowen, president, to the same purchaser.[9] The resultant network of Southland Greyhound Lines provided routes from San Antonio to Corpus Christi via Sinton, San Antonio to Victoria via Nixon, San Antonio to Lake Charles via Houston and Beaumont, San Antonio to Fort Worth and Dallas via Austin and Waco, Dallas to San Angelo via Cisco and Coleman, Dallas to El Paso via Abilene and Big Spring, and Dallas to Lamesa via Mineral Wells and Snyder, with branches off this last route to Graham (from Mineral Wells) and Stamford (from Albany).

In effecting the merger leading to Southland Greyhound Lines, Bowen and the other Texas operators were following a national trend. In May of 1929, pursuant to a February agreement between Greyhound and Yelloway, four of the most important bus systems in the nation had merged to provide a gigantic coast-to-coast network. The four parties to the thirty-million-dollar merger were Yelloway, Greyhound, Pickwick Stages of Los Angeles, and the Southern Pacific Railroad.[10] Greyhound emerged as the dominant partner in the new corporation, gaining control of the routes of Yelloway, Pickwick, and Southern Pacific Motor Transport for a price of twelve million dollars.[11]

Edward C. Eckstrom, who was to become the first president and general manager of Southland Greyhound Lines, had founded an early bus line in Chicago that ran to various communities in Michigan. Eckstrom had then joined Carl Eric Wickman, Ralph Bogan, and Orville S. Caesar in forming the Northland Transportation Company to consolidate bus service in Illinois, Michigan,

Minnesota, and Wisconsin.[12] Eckstrom moved to Texas in 1927 and began operating service between Dallas and Fort Worth, soon expanding from Dallas to Austin via Waco through acquisition of the Parker Motor Line. He formed the Southland–Red Ball Motor Bus Company in 1927 and expanded the service to include Waco–Fort Worth, Austin–Temple, Fort Worth–Laredo, and Austin–San Antonio.[13] It was this organization that merged with the Bowen interests in 1929 to form Southland Greyhound Lines.

Ed Eckstrom subsequently left the bus business and purchased the Yellow Cab Company in San Antonio, but the Greyhound presence in Texas continued to grow in scope and influence. The Southland Greyhound Lines became Southwestern Greyhound Lines on September 25, 1933, as part of a national reorganization of routes and structures by the parent company. On October 1, 1933, Southwestern Greyhound acquired the Southwestern Transportation Company, the subsidiary of the Cotton Belt Railroad that had bought out W. E. Nunnelee in 1928.[14]

Commissioners Smith, Terrell, and Ernest O. Thompson approved the transfer of specific Certificates of Convenience and Necessity in an order dated November 1, 1933, thus officially transferring all principal routes from Southland Greyhound Lines to Southwestern Greyhound Lines.[15] The Greyhound unit in Texas remained Southwestern Greyhound Lines, with headquarters in Fort Worth, from September, 1933 throughout the postwar period. Operating through "friendly affiliates" such as the Kerrville Bus Company, Southwestern Greyhound became and remained one of the most influential and active lines in Texas intercity bus history through the end of World War II.

The Kerrville Bus Company

One of the major independent companies to emerge and survive during the late twenties was the Kerrville Bus Company, an efficient, well-managed intercity bus line, which still provides service throughout much of Texas. The history of this company is of special interest because it includes the first full-scale dispute adjudicated

This Pickwick–Greyhound Lines "Nite Coach," a "pullman of the highways," was supposed to revolutionize motorbus travel in the 1930s but failed to find a real audience. Although the "Morpheus," named for the ancients' god of slumber, was photographed here in the snows of Chicago, Greyhound did attempt some limited "Nite Coach" service in Texas for a short time. J. C. Carrington.

by the Railroad Commission involving making permanent the temporary certificates and permits issued under the grandfather clause in 1927.

At the time of regulation a triumvirate of bus lines plied between San Antonio and Kerrville, all operating converted automobiles.[16] The Railroad Commission had granted temporary permits to J. L. and J. A. Power for five and a half trips per day, to Hal Peterson for two and a half trips daily, and to Union Bus Company for two additional round-trips daily. In the summer of 1927, all three permit holders filed for permanent certificates, with Union Bus Company protesting any permanent rights for the Power and Peterson families, and the Powers and Hal Peterson protesting any awarding of certificates to the Union Bus Company.

Because the hearing involved the first major dispute of franchise rights under the Beck Bus Law, the Railroad Commission took extensive testimony, consolidated the three applications into a single case, and staged the first hearing at Kerrville on August 26, 1927. Another hearing convened in Austin on August 28, and a final session occurred at Kerrville on October 1, 1927.

During the course of the hearings, evidence was introduced to show that J. L. Power had begun service between Kerrville and San Antonio in August of 1921. By 1925 the Union Bus Company had added service of its own, and also in 1925 Hal Peterson had purchased two Buick sedans and had begun service over the same route. A mutual agreement had been reached that stabilized the service at ten round-trips a day, divided as indicated among the Power family, Hal Peterson, and the Union Bus Company.[17]

During the hearings the Union Bus Company contended that Peterson and Power were actually operating as its agents while driving their schedules, that they had used the Union Terminal in San Antonio, displayed the Union Bus Company flag on their vehicles, paid a charge of one dollar per departure from the San Antonio terminal, and otherwise acted as subsidiary operators for the company. Union Bus Company contended that it alone was therefore the owner of the franchises.

Peterson and Power saw their relationship with Union to be quite different from the interpretation placed on it by the company. They acknowledged the fees paid to Union and the use of the company flag and terminal facilities, but stated that they had retained separate identities primarily because they, not the Union Bus Company, were liable for damages to passengers or property incurred on their runs. They also pointed to Union's two separate schedules per day as prima facie evidence that a distinction existed between their operations and those of the company.[18]

On December 3, 1927, the commission held that J. L. and J. A. Power and Hal Peterson had operated their schedules in good faith prior to January 11, 1927, not as agents of the Union Bus Company but as private independent operators. The ruling stipulated that Union be given permanent certificates between San Antonio and Kerrville for only two daily round-trips, not the ten that the company sought, and that the Powers and Peterson should divide the other eight so that half runs would be eliminated. In other words, the commission found that, although "the Union Bus Company has performed a commendable and useful service to the public in furnishing a central place for the arrival and departure of motor passenger vehicles," this service did not entitle the company to absolute permanent rights that would harm the independent operators who had used the company facilities.[19] The commission order thus dismissed all of the filed protests and made permanent the temporary certificates over the several objections of the competing lines.

Hal Peterson bought out the Amberson and Power interests, formed the Kerrville Bus Company in 1929, and was soon in full control of intercity bus service in the Hill Country. At the time of the formation of the company, according to veteran executive Guy Griggs, the main road was paved to a point nineteen miles west of San Antonio, and the pavement commenced again about eight miles east of Kerrville. The standard running time in 1929 was two and a half hours, but that time required optimum road conditions. The highway traversed countless low-water crossings, and frequently the Packards and Buicks were unable to plunge through the rushing waters of swollen Hill Country streams.[20]

On March 29, 1929, the Railroad Commission approved the sale and transfer of certificates from the Union Bus Company (Miller Pendleton and James Amberson) to the Union Bus Lines (Joe Amberson) for operation between San Antonio and San Angelo.[21] This route, as well as service northwest from San Angelo to Big Spring and a line from Brady to Abilene via Santa Anna, ultimately joined the Kerrville system in 1938.[22]

Hal Peterson, Guy Griggs, Henry Mathews, J. D. Mahaffey, and other executives steered a solidly expanding course for the Kerrville Bus Company. They obtained operating rights from Kerrville to Junction in 1929, from Austin to Houston in 1930, from Austin to Kerrville in

These Fitzjohn sedans were freshly painted and ready for service on Union Bus Lines in the mid-1930s. The obvious spare tires and the running boards have disappeared, and the baggage racks are now an integral part of the streamlined appearance of the sedans. Motor Bus Society.

1933, and from Austin to Victoria via Lockhart, over the route pioneered by Josh Merritt, in 1936.[23]

Even while it retained its independence, however, Kerrville Bus Company built a strong alliance with Greyhound, operating from Greyhound terminals in San Antonio, Houston, and Austin and leasing the line from Junction to Pecos from Southland and then from Southwestern Greyhound Lines until well after the end of the Second World War.

Kerrville was later destined to purchase the complete operation of the Painter Bus Line, headquartered in Uvalde and owned by the colorful Walter R. Painter, an Australian who developed a solid business in the Winter Garden area. Many old-timers in the bus business recall that Painter's wife, Allura, paid scrupulous attention to the interior of Painter vehicles, personally repairing seat covers and sewing on headrests. By the mid-thirties the Painter Bus Lines served lines from Del Rio to San Antonio and south from Uvalde to Crystal City and Carrizo Springs.

This converted Chrysler Airflow sedan illustrates Union Bus Lines' desire for increased passenger capacity and the trend toward streamlining transportation vehicles. Note the fashionable decorations on the side of the hood, the streamlined hood ornament, and the decorated covering over the rear tires. Motor Bus Society.

Airline Motor Coaches

Meanwhile, in East Texas the type of merger encouraged by the Beck Bus Law was taking place. George Wellington Hyde had founded a line between Huntsville and Houston in 1927.[24] C. D. Thomas's Thomas Motor Coaches were carrying passengers and express between Lufkin and Livingston, and Clarence T. English's Red Ball Bus Line was serving such communities as Lufkin, Garrison, and Nacogdoches.[25] Thomas and English saw the advantages of merger and formed Air Line Motor Coaches (later spelled "Airline") on April 17, 1930. The Houston, Humble, and Livingston Bus Line, of which Hyde was a partner, joined Airline in 1931, and a rapid pace of mergers and acquisitions continued throughout the thirties. Other routes absorbed included the Fite and Wallace Line into Longview in 1931; the leasing of rights between Henderson and Tyler from Sunshine Bus Lines in 1933; Bill's Bus Line between Gladewater and Tyler via Kilgore and Arp in 1935; and the Red Star Bus Line between Marshall and Beaumont in 1937. Still more ac-

The Kerrville Bus Company acquired through rights between Austin and Houston via Giddings and Brenham in 1930. The destination sign reads "Special," and the uniform of operator McGee looks brand new in this photograph commemorating the new service. Kerrville Bus Company, Inc.

quisitions brought Monzingo Bus Lines into the Airline structure in 1938, thereby adding an attractive alternate route into Shreveport, Louisiana. The company kept adding lines right through the beginning of World War II, acquiring rights and equipment from small carriers that provided Airline feeder routes to such points as Brenham, Huntsville, Trinity, and Navasota.[26]

Airline was a profitable and efficient company from its inception until its sale to Dixie–Sunshine Trailways of Dallas in 1946. The report of the company at the close of business on December 31, 1935, indicated 420 miles of regular routes operated and annual receipts of $178,749.28.[27] Net income for 1934 had been $27,760;

Passengers board the schedule for Houston in the Austin Greyhound terminal in the summer of 1939. Shortly, the terminals and coaches of Texas would be jammed with soldiers and others set in motion by the war. Kerrville Bus Company, Inc.

in 1945 it had risen to a robust $780,492. Dixie-Sunshine paid $1.5 million for the company on December 10, 1946.[28]

G. W. Hyde sold his interests in Airline Motor Coaches and moved to Cleburne in 1933, where he began an operation to become known as Central Texas Bus Line. Hyde purchased this line from J. C. Duvall, the Fort Worth representative active in TBOA affairs, and a partner named Sam Canuteson, who told him that he could have an old Cadillac they were operating if he would purchase the tires for cash and finish off the payments of the vehicle. Although the asking price of the line was originally twenty thousand dollars, Hyde purchased it for only fifty-two hundred dollars. He began operations with two vehicles running between Fort Worth and Cleburne in March, 1933.[29]

Hyde steadily increased his operations, eventually

At the courthouse in Uvalde in 1937, Painter Bus Lines coach #14 dwarfs the Uvalde–San Antonio sedan alongside it. Note the Greyhound dog used as a hood ornament on the sedan. J. C. Carrington.

adding lines from Cleburne to Dallas via Alvarado, Cleburne to Temple via Clifton and McGregor (parallel to the track of the Santa Fe Railroad), and from Cleburne to Corsicana via Hillsboro. Before absorbing Sam Day's Bee Line Coaches, Central Texas was known as Cleburne–Fort Worth Motor Coaches, but Hyde thought the name Central Texas Bus Line better represented the scope of the enterprise.

The Industry at Mid-Decade

The Congress of the United States passed the Motor Carrier Act in 1935 and thus brought all bus lines engaged in interstate operations under the control of the Interstate Commerce Commission (ICC).[30] Because bus operations had been effectively regulated by the Motor Transportation Division of the Railroad Commission for

This portrait of the Airline Motor Coaches staff, taken in Nacogdoches about 1936, includes drivers, mechanics, company president C. D. Thomas (back row, fifth from left), superintendent H. O. Hooker (back row, third from right), and even the mascot. G. W. Hyde.

some eight years, however, the effect on Texas' intercity bus lines was minimal. Another level of the government now became involved in the regulatory process, however, and companies operating across the borders into neighboring states found somewhat longer delays in getting their applications approved. In addition, the law was interpreted in such a way that any carrier accepting tickets or waybills of another carrier engaged in interstate traffic came under the definition of an interstate rather than an intrastate operation and thus under the jurisdiction of the federal law. Airline Motor Coaches, for instance, had to receive ICC approval for its 1940 petition to operate over a connecting distance of just nineteen miles between Trinity and Huntsville, because Airline did business in another state, Louisiana, and with other carriers that did business in other states.[31]

After selling to Southland Greyhound Lines in 1929, R. C. Bowen had remained active in the industry and had rebuilt a route system to compete with the Southland structure. By March of 1936, Bowen Motor Coaches was, after Southwestern Greyhound, the largest operator in Texas. Bowen's 1935 payroll was $230,381 on a total personnel roster of 183 workers, and state and local taxes for the year stood at $63,072.19.[32] Bowen Motor Coaches commanded a route structure of 2,089 miles in early 1936, with the major runs being from Fort Worth–Dallas to Houston, Dallas to Wichita Falls and on to Amarillo, Fort Worth to San Angelo via Brownwood, and Houston to Corpus Christi.

From his headquarters in Fort Worth, Bowen told an interviewer for *Bus Transportation* in 1935 that his two rules of operation had been to "make the fare attractive" and to "improve the service regardless of cost."[33] Bowen became somewhat famous in the bus business for his policy of immediately rebating fares on any unused tickets and for his instructions to agents to accept without question the claim of any passenger who purported to have lost his or her ticket.

Bowen remained an ardent advocate of government regulation and actively supported the 1935 Motor Carrier Act. His enthusiasm for the federal legislation recalls his earlier efforts in behalf of the TBOA with Guy Shields and J. C. Carrington: "The bus men should be proud that this has been brought about through their own untiring efforts. It is as though the Congress who has enacted the law has said to the bus operator, 'Go ahead, boys, we're with you. Your principle is right.'"[34]

Bowen moved to consolidate his position still further in late 1937 and petitioned the ICC to merge all of the related lines he then controlled—such companies as Lone Star Stage Lines, Fort Worth–Corsicana–Mexia Coaches, and Roberson Bus Lines—into the parent organization, with all lines to become known as Bowen Motor Coaches. The effective date of the name change and the subsequent liquidation of the smaller lines was January 1,

This White-Bender model exhibits all the hallmarks of the streamlined era, which was at its height in about 1936: decorative arrows, "teardrop" designs on mud flaps and wheel covers, the White name and logo at the center of the wheels, and liberal use of running lights. Motor Bus Society.

1938.[35] Bowen Motor Coaches, sold in 1943, was to form a major part of the nucleus of the Trailways system.

Another vital component of the Trailways network was Dixie–Sunshine Trailways, an outgrowth of the Dixie Motor Coach Corporation and Sunshine Bus Lines. J. C. Riter wrote in 1943 that the Sunshine Bus Lines began operations shortly after World War I:

> In 1919, we started the Sunshine Bus Lines, Inc., with one old Model T broken down car, operating more or less at intervals when we could get passengers between Terrell and Dallas. We eventually started another operation between Terrell and Grand Saline and extended that operation into Mineola and eventually into Tyler. . . . We had no roads over which to travel and we had no particular schedules to be maintained—no ticket systems

or anything like that. We just simply operated up and down the road on four schedules a day and got to our destinations when we could, according to the weather conditions.[36]

A. W. Riter of Sunshine Bus Lines purchased all of the capital stock of the Dixie Motor Coach Corporation in 1931. The two companies were brought together under a single roof in Dallas in 1934, but Sunshine continued to operate Dixie as a separate corporation until after the war.[37]

At mid-decade, therefore, the bus industry in Texas was by some measures strong and prospering. A contemporary report listed 108 bus lines in the Texas market, operating 19,955 route miles and carrying more than five million passengers. The largest companies, in order, were Southwestern Greyhound, Bowen Motor Coaches, and Kerrville Bus Company. Other companies accorded importance at mid-decade, in addition to the Dixie-Sunshine system, were Painter Bus Lines of Uvalde, the various forerunners of Central Texas Bus Line, Airline Motor Coaches, and Union Bus Lines, along with a host of smaller operations. The Creamer Stage Line of Eastland, founded by pioneer Louis Hardy Creamer, was still operating in 1936, but destined to sell out to R. C. Bowen two years later. And the western section of the state was the province of McMakin Motor Coaches of Lubbock, Panhandle Stages of Amarillo, and Red Star Coaches of Vernon.[38]

On the eastern side of the state, the Missouri Pacific Transportation Company, the highway subsidiary of the Missouri Pacific Railroad, continued to expand throughout the thirties. Missouri Pacific Transportation purchased rights from Texarkana to Marshall from South Texas Coaches in May of 1930 and from Marshall to Palestine from Bee Line Coaches that same month. The company began through service from St. Louis and Memphis to Palestine on July 1, 1930.[39] Extended service between Palestine and Huntsville followed in August of 1931, and Missouri Pacific buses thereafter began operating directly into Houston over the rights of South Texas Coaches, later Bowen Motor Coaches. There was little Missouri Pacific expansion in Texas during the rest of the prewar period, although the line did acquire a few

This Studebaker of the Missouri Pacific Transportation Company is, like its driver, at ease in Brownsville in the summer of 1931. The narrow window on the passenger's side and the half window behind the driver are open for ventilation on this hot day. Motor Bus Society.

additional rights in Arkansas and Louisiana in the mid-thirties.

Despite its fairly limited route system in Texas before the war, however, the Missouri Pacific Transportation Company had a major role to play in the development of the Texas bus industry. When the ICC took a hand in the interstate regulation of the motorbus industry, the bus subsidiaries of the railroads found themselves in an awkward position. The legislation authorizing ICC approval called on the railroads to use their highway subsidiaries to strengthen rather than compete against the railroad's passenger services. In addition to facing this restriction, the railroads recognized the ferocious competitive campaign being waged by the Greyhound organization. In November of 1935, therefore, the western bus subsidiaries of three major railroads—Santa Fe, Burlington, and Missouri Pacific—began discussions that resulted in forming a voluntary association to be known as the National Trailways Bus System.[40] Paul J. Neff, vice-president and general manager of the Missouri Pacific Transportation Company, was a prime mover in the development and founding of Trailways and quickly converted the subsidiary into Missouri Pacific Trailways. During the war and the postwar recovery, Trailways was to use part of the original Missouri Pacific network as a major component of its giant Texas route system.

Economic Effects of the Depression

Despite the robust signs of life in the Texas bus industry as witnessed in the 1936 report of the ICC and the 1935 report of Airline Motor Coaches, the Great Depression did have some adverse economic consequences in the industry. Lines that were lightly patronized tended to disappear, such as the Missouri Pacific's short-lived branch from Marshall into Dallas. Small operators who could not effectively merge with another company found themselves unable to get operating loans and were forced to sell out or simply to shut down. The larger corporations were expanding everywhere, and the smaller operators were beginning to leave the business. Those with ready cash, like G. W. Hyde, found someone like Sam Canuteson more than ready to settle for a final sale price well below the asking figure. Many sold out too soon, in the opinion of Hyde, and would have made good money had they been able to hang on until the war turned the bus industry around.[41]

Like other industries nationwide, the bus industry at first believed that the Depression would soon be over. In a June, 1930, editorial in *Bus Transportation*, Carl Stocks, editor of the journal, advised busmen this way: "All signs point to recovery from the current business depression before winter. . . . While a rapid resumption of normal business is not immediately expected, a rather definite upward trend may be looked for soon, with the normal level achieved by October." Stocks went on to admonish his readers not to despair but rather to look toward a brighter day: "The bus industry has not felt the current depression as much as other forms of transportation and business in general. This is all the more reason for it to disregard pessimistic advice. It should strike out with confidence in its plans for the future. By so doing it will benefit itself and help industry as a whole get back to normal."[42]

The realities of the situation, however, were somewhat different. Passengers who did not have to travel generally stayed home. The agricultural areas of Texas, Oklahoma, and Arkansas lost much of their population during this period, thereby, of course, reducing the aggregate number of potential bus travelers. R. C. Bowen and the Kerrville Bus Company and G. W. Hyde and others with ready money found excellent bargains and added to their networks, but many smaller operations gave up.

One type of smaller operation that did fare rather well during this period, however, was the short-run commuter line. Texas Bus Lines operated from a solid base of commuter business in Galveston and Houston and counted on a large volume of passengers going to and from work in communities like Texas City, Dickinson, League City, and LaMarque. The commuter-style Beaumont–Port Arthur Bus Line provided various discount plans for frequent riders and functioned much like a city transit line, as did the Texas Motorcoaches operation between Fort Worth and Dallas. Webb Greer's Bay Shore Bus Lines also operated a successful commuter business between Houston and Goose Creek.

As the thirties drew to a close, a major new company came into existence in West Texas with the merger of South Plains Coaches and the McMakin Motor Coaches into Texas, New Mexico, and Oklahoma Coaches, Inc. The ICC authorized the new corporation on May 31, 1939. A condition of the merger was that all stock of the predecessor companies be canceled and their charters forfeited. Grover C. McMakin retained only 6 percent of the new corporation; the largest share held by one individual was the 36.5 percent in the name of R. C. Bowen,

ACF, a Philadelphia manufacturer with moderately strong ties to the Texas market, produced Texas Bus Lines #204, something of a cross between a transit bus and an intercity coach, in 1940. Note the multiple window compartments that surround the driver and the accordion door more typical of transit buses. Motor Bus Society.

although controlling interest was vested in the 38 percent held by Mr. and Mrs. Joe Bowman.[43]

Meanwhile, the Bus Division of the Texas Motor Transportation Association remained relatively active in securing the rights of the bus operators, although there continued to be a feeling that the TMTA had moved rather far away from the interests of the state's bus lines. The Bus Division met at 2:30 P.M. on June 15, 1939, at the Rice Hotel in Houston, during the fifth annual TMTA convention. Chairman R. C. Bowen conducted the meeting, and the list of agencies represented accurately reflects the relative influence of the bus lines at this time: Bowen Motor Coaches; Airline Motor Coaches; Bee Line Coaches; Southwestern Greyhound Lines; Texas Bus Lines of Galveston; Panhandle Motor

THE DEPRESSION AND THE COMING OF THE WAR

Twin Coach built this thirty-seven-passenger model for Texas Motorcoaches in 1937. Received by TMC in 1938, #1622 is thought to have been the last of its kind delivered to a U.S. bus line for intercity service. Motor Bus Society.

Coaches of Amarillo; Mack's Motor Coaches of Crockett; Kerrville Bus Company; and a representative of the ICC.[44] Although the TBOA had similarly been influenced in earlier days by a rather small number of active participants, some of the personnel had obviously changed in the intervening years. Joe C. Carrington, no longer directly associated with the Bus Division, did not attend the meeting.

The TMTA seemed interested in assisting the bus operators but unsure as to how to proceed. TMTA secretary B. Frank Johnson, for example, spoke to the meeting and "urged that the operators meet with the other officials of the TMTA and advise the organization of what it wanted done so that every effort could be made to give entire satisfaction." After Johnson's departure, however, R. C. Bowen led a discussion about this invita-

The Beaumont–Port Arthur Bus Line schedule for December, 1938–January, 1939, illustrates the patronage and demand level for bus service at the end of the thirties. The minimum one-way fare that the line would handle was ten cents. Motor Bus Society.

tion with the following, rather predictable, result: "The consensus of opinion was that the matters now most pertinent before the bus division were problems that they alone could work out. That, while they were too weak to stand alone as a separate organization and needed the strength of the Texas Motor Transportation Association, their problems were individual as to their division."[45]

Other matters of concern to the operators present on June 15 were the battle with travel bureaus (which had recently come into existence and were being used as clearinghouses for passengers who needed cheaper fares than the bus lines provided), an improved system for handling schedule changes before the commission, and the need for more regular meetings of the bus operators. Guy Griggs, the first president and chairman of the board of Kerrville, proposed these regular meetings and invited the operators to Hal Peterson's Diamond Bar Ranch for the weekend of July 7, 1939.[46]

By the time of the next convention of the TMTA in Tyler in May of 1940, Texas and the nation were moving into a prewar mentality. A committee of busmen had been organized by the TMTA and the Bus Division to continue the discussion of travel bureau regulation, and C. D. Thomas dutifully called a meeting on May 16 at which such regulation, along with the question of carrier liability, was perfunctorily discussed.[47] The questions of franchises and insurance were beginning to seem secondary, as the state and the nation began to emerge from the Great Depression and to watch the storm clouds gathering over Europe. Soon the intercity bus industry would be so busy that neither drivers nor owners would have time to do much more than get the buses loaded and somehow, some way, move down the road.

4. The War and the Postwar Transition

World War II had a profound effect on the Texas intercity bus industry. Most of the bus manufacturers saw their plants converted to wartime production for military needs. Parts were scarce, and qualified mechanics were in demand by the armed forces. The War Production Board and the Office of Defense Transportation curtailed many expendable routes and requisitioned the buses. Despite these restrictions, however, the bus lines of the state and the nation handled a vastly increased load of passengers.

Both drivers and passengers who recall this era remember the hectic commotion of depots, the frequent breakdowns on the highway, and the general agony involved in getting anywhere. Soldiers were willing to ride in luggage racks and baggage bins to get to a larger town on a weekend pass. Mothers, wives, and girlfriends of servicemen traveled patiently across the state to spend even a few moments with the soldiers. Passenger loads were frequently "standing room only," and extraordinary delays in allegedly "scheduled" departures were routine. One veteran driver told of pulling into the San Antonio depot in 1943, only to have the press of humanity rip the entrance door off the bus, causing a two-hour delay of his already-tardy departure for Dallas.[1]

All lines were busy during the war years, but especially hectic were those that served the numerous military installations around the state: Arrow Coach Lines into Camp Bowie, Dixie-Sunshine into Camp Runnels and Camp Fannin, Bowen Motor Coaches also into Camp Bowie, and all the lines serving El Paso, Corpus Christi, San Antonio, and other nerve centers of the military establishment. The large number of military bases in Texas gave increased prominence to the intercity bus industry of the state, and civilian travel also escalated because of

George Wellington Hyde's Cleburne–Fort Worth Bus Line had recently been renamed Central Texas Bus Lines when it took delivery of this Flxible twenty-five-passenger coach in 1941. Bus #6 features chrome crossbars across the front, which were a Flxible staple on most models until after the war. The air horns were an extra twenty-five dollars at this time. Motor Bus Society.

such wartime measures as gasoline and tire rationing.

Civilian travel, of course, frequently suffered from government demands on the bus operators' limited resources: a vehicle pressed into Office of Defense Transportation (ODT) service simply was one less vehicle to transport civilians. Priority for equipment and drivers was naturally granted to the government, and the bus industry responded quickly and patriotically to most requests.

The statistics on nationwide bus travel during the war years reveal impressive growth and development. In 1939 all intercity buses traveled a total of 8.7 billion passenger miles. In 1941 the figure had risen to 13.7 billion, and by 1944 the U.S. intercity bus line industry traveled 32.9 billion passenger miles for the year.[2] Texas was proportionately affected in terms of bus ridership.

A large number of travelers were service personnel,

Clarence E. Roberson's Arrow Coach Lines was a huge success, due in part to the presence of Camp Bowie at Brownwood, the hub of company operations. This twenty-nine-passenger Flxible coach became part of the Arrow fleet in the summer of 1944. Motor Bus Society.

and their travel demands placed a further burden on the industry: "The bulk of weekend transportation during the war was for service men, most of whom were on leave. The problem of bus companies handling service men was made doubly difficult by the fact that all of them seemed to leave at almost the same time, being compelled to report back to their respective stations at the same time. This factor meant that many schedules had to be made up into as many as 15 or 20 sections."[3]

Other problems of wartime also plagued the bus lines: communications were still rather primitive in many areas, and breakdowns largely went unreported; highway repairs were frequently neglected unless the roads were major arteries deemed necessary for wartime emergency;

roads were often closed suddenly because of military maneuvers in the area; national and regional meetings of bus operators were suspended during the war effort, with exceptions made only for those meetings summoned by the Office of Defense Transportation; since paper was at a premium, even features such as the "Ticket Window" and "Bus Chatter" in *Motor Transportation* were suspended because they did not directly support the war effort.

All of these problems were put into perspective by Adam Sledz, who served as assistant comptroller of Greyhound during the war:

> Our biggest problem was the scarcity of materials during the war. We could not get the parts we needed, which meant that a good many buses were laid up for repairs. As for the delivery of new coaches on order, they were so badly delayed that in some civilian areas we had to curtail schedules. Worst of all was the manpower problem. More than 4,000 of our drivers, maintenance men, and other employees went into the armed forces. It was no easy task to replace them.[4]

The problem of scarce materials was indeed real. Greyhound was not alone in its inability to get adequate replacement parts, and even its policy of stockpiling and preventive maintenance could not overcome a demand increase that quadrupled in the first year of the war. The manpower shortage at the factories was a wartime reality, and Greyhound could not get parts from General Motors because General Motors could not get sufficient components from its suppliers: "The Ferro Foundry and Machine Company in Cleveland operated at sixty percent; the Standard Foundry in Racine at fifty percent; Gell Manufacturing of Albion, Michigan, at sixty percent; and United Brass and Aluminum, in Port Huron, Michigan, sixty percent."[5]

With parts production at a near standstill and new orders delayed or suspended "for the duration," many companies in Texas and the rest of the nation turned to older equipment and simply "made do"—a condition that contributed to the numerous highway breakdowns. Drivers, ticket agents, maintenance men, and buses were pressed into service for the emergency:

Photographed on the Texas Bus Lines lot in Galveston, this wartime model, #252, eliminates all pretense to intercity travel. The White-built city-style bus has no curtains and no reclining seats. Motor Bus Society.

Hundreds of elderly buses slated for retirement were refurbished, repainted, and put back into traffic. Production of heavy-duty buses was slowed and then ceased altogether as large factories were turned over to war production. Lightweight school buses and stretched out sedans continued to be made available by the War Production Board, and quite a few major intercity carriers had to supplement their luxurious parlor coaches with these much less pretentious vehicles.[6]

One of the few manufacturers allowed to continue any significant volume of intercity bus production was the Beck Company of Sidney, Ohio. Hal Peterson had formed a partnership with C. D. Beck in the 1930s by which the Petersons owned a third interest in the Beck Company, Beck owned another third, and Ohio and Texas bankers controlled the remaining third.[7] The Kerrville Bus Company was, throughout the history of Beck bus production, a major Texas purchaser of these buses for intercity transportation. This arrangement continued beyond the war years and brought a large number of Beck buses into the Texas market.

Kerrville was not alone in its use of Becks. Most Texas bus lines had little choice during World War II because Beck was at least able to supply a few new buses to the industry. While it was true that Beck was not converted to wartime production of military equipment and could continue to produce coaches, its wartime output did not match its normal standards:

> These buses left much to be desired on the road and in the shop. The riding quality was among the worst. Road calls were frequent, and the buses were underpowered. The mechanics [at Airline Motor Coaches] did not like to work on them due to the non-standardized components, such as brakes. In all fairness to Beck, most of the deficiencies in these vehicles can probably be traced to the lack of parts and components available to Beck for manufacturing into a bus. Beck buses otherwise held a highly satisfactory judgment in the eyes of many, many bus lines over the years.[8]

The buses provided to Airline, Kerrville, Painter, Bowen, and others by the Beck Company were generally the stripped-down "Mainliner" models with a thirty-three-passenger capacity. They were purchased in numbers as large as wartime regulations would permit between 1942 and 1947 and became a staple of the Texas intercity bus industry during the war and postwar recovery.

Equipment and maintenance problems were heightened for the Texas bus lines, as they were for the rest of the nation, by a phenomenally accelerated rate of passenger demand. After gasoline and other forms of rationing were imposed, traffic increased rapidly, and the operators frequently ran schedules as soon as equipment became available and with little regard for the number of passengers that had to be crowded into a coach. One veteran driver recalls heading out of Wichita Falls with sixty-two passengers on a twenty-nine-passenger bus.[9] Airline reported loads of up to one hundred passengers on a bus built to accommodate thirty-seven.[10] Most lines regretted the conditions but realized that people had to reach their destinations, and in general the passengers understood the exigencies of wartime travel: "Drivers

This stripped-down model, a Bowen Mainliner (1941), was typical of wartime buses produced by the Beck Company of Sidney, Ohio. Even the headlights look stark. Motor Bus Society.

were instructed to always allow a passenger to board if there was half enough room. Servicemen always had priority. It wasn't uncommon for Nacogdoches-Houston schedules to have as many as seven sections, due to the development of Nacogdoches as a major transfer point."[11]

One of the other major transporters of huge numbers of servicemen in the war years in Texas was Arrow Coach Lines, which had been organized by Clarence Roberson, R. M. Belcher, and B. U. Ross under an oral agreement of partnership in September of 1935. Arrow Coach Lines ultimately transported thousands of soldiers and dependents millions of bus miles during World War II due in large measure to its effective management and the key location of its headquarters in Brownwood, a major east-west junction of both rail and highway transportation. Brownwood was also the site of Camp Bowie, one of the largest and most active of the military installations in the state.

This photograph is postwar (November 22, 1963, when National Guardsmen were on maneuvers at Fort Hood) but gives the flavor of World War II troop movements. During the war the bus lines were so busy, hardly anyone had time to take pictures. Arrow Coach Lines.

On September 6, 1935, B. U. Ross as an individual officially transferred all rights from Brownwood to Austin and Brownwood to Waco to Ross Motor Coaches, a partnership comprising himself, Roberson, and Belcher.[12] Ross had acquired these and other rights from the Kerrville Bus Company on February 9 and February 13, 1933.[13] Clarence Roberson, critically ill from 1932 until his death in 1941, had dubbed the new company Arrow Coach Lines because he thought its routes from Brownwood to Waco and Austin ran as "straight as an arrow."[14]

There was little development of the Arrow route structure during the war. Most hearings on certificates were, like so much else, suspended for the duration, and the operators were preoccupied with wartime problems. One of the few hearings concerning Arrow during this period allowed through service from Austin to Briggs over the new highway "with closed doors between Austin and Leander," a procedure that saved Arrow about ten miles per trip.[15]

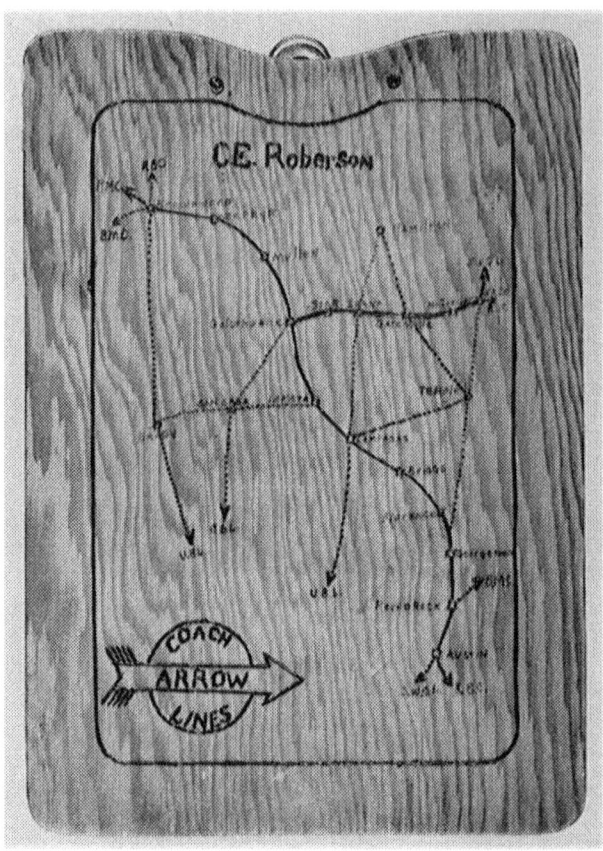

Clarence Roberson was quite ill when he founded Arrow Coach Lines just before World War II and carved this system map of the route "straight as an arrow" on the back of his clipboard. Roberson died in 1941. Alice Roberson Cofer.

Immediately after the war, Arrow Coach Lines became more aggressive in acquisitions. On August 7, 1945, it purchased from B. U. Ross the rights from Brownwood to Cross Plains via Cross Cut and thus secured a shorter through route to Abilene.[16] Two weeks later it purchased rights to the Belton-Lometa-Brady service from the descendants of Louis Hardy Creamer and thus secured rights into Killeen and Camp Hood.[17] Orders of the Railroad Commission issued on January 22, 1946, consolidated the Arrow structure and granted permanent certificates for a network that reached through the heart of Texas from Waco and Hearne and Austin into Abilene.[18] Ultimately, in March of 1946, the partners of Arrow Coach Lines drew up an agreement to replace a set of handshakes that had guided the bus line for eleven years. As the postwar era began, the principal owners (62 percent of the stock) were Mrs. Alice R. Cofer (the wife of the deceased Clarence E. Roberson) and her daughter, Mrs. M. O. Killion; the other two owners were original partner R. M. Belcher and his son Robert.[19]

In their policy of little change during the war years, the partners in Arrow Coach Lines were repeating a pattern found around the state. World War II was so demanding that most operators thought little of expansion. Panhandle Stages of Amarillo, for instance, had embarked on a solidly aggressive campaign of route additions during the Depression, but was pretty well dormant in its structural changes between 1938 and 1949.[20] The Kerrville Bus Company had acquired the bulk of its wartime route structure by 1939 and made no significant changes until just before the end of the war. Southwestern Greyhound Lines, similarly, had few alterations during this wartime period, although it did lease its operation from Mineral Wells to Jacksboro and Graham to Kemp Bus Lines and John Kemp for five years beginning January 1, 1942. The terms of the agreement between Kemp and Greyhound called for Kemp Bus Lines to pay Greyhound half of the excess revenues over eleven cents a mile.[21]

One operator who remained fairly active in acquisition and development throughout the war years, however, was R. C. Bowen of Bowen Motor Coaches. Bowen filed numerous applications during this period, frequently for extensions and development of service or for rearrangement of his corporate structure. He was always alert to business opportunities. When Camp Bowie opened three miles southwest of Brownwood in the fall of 1940, J. S. Folkner of the Brownwood-Brady Bus Line was simply unable to cope with the sharply increased demand along his forty-six-mile route. Bowen leased the Brownwood-Brady operation from Folkner for a four-year period from November 15, 1940, through November 14, 1944, with an option to re-lease the line for another four years in 1944.[22] It was a highly lucrative arrangement.

In 1943 Bowen formed a Tennessee holding company

One of the few Texas bus accidents involving fatalities occurred about midnight on May 21, 1942. The driver of a stolen car had reportedly been drinking and drove his vehicle into the front of the Bowen bus with tremendous and fatal impact. The accident took place on a rain-slick road in a sparsely populated area near Claude in the Panhandle. Texas State Archives/Department of Public Safety Collection.

known as Lone Star Coaches, Inc., for the purpose of transferring all of his assets to the more favorable corporate laws of that state. Bowen Motor Coaches was totally owned at the time of transfer by R. C. Bowen, and all stock in Bowen Motor Coaches was sold to Lone Star. A major reason for this maneuver lay in Bowen's attempts to secure what he perceived to be a highly attractive route from Amarillo to Denver, which would extend his Dallas-Amarillo service into Colorado. After being denied his petition to purchase the Amarillo-Denver Bus Company from W. H. Woodlief on February 4, 1943, Bowen effected this corporate reorganization and saw his request granted

This Bowen coach destined for Dallas was produced by White and probably delivered to the line in 1942. It saw service on Bowen's commuter lines radiating from Dallas to such points as Irving, Euless, Pleasant Mound, and Pleasant Grove. Motor Bus Society.

by the ICC on December 4, 1944. Sale price for the 422-mile route was just fifteen hundred dollars, the "bargain basement" price evidently resulting from Woodlief's inability to obtain equipment to operate over the line.[23] Other Bowen extensions during the war included the rights from Mexia to Hillsboro and from Mount Enterprise to Carthage in 1943, from Olney to Stamford in 1944, and from Eastland to Stamford and Amarillo to Tucumcari in the spring of 1945.[24]

Bowen had affiliated with Trailways in 1943, and immediately after the war the Bowen network became an integral part of the newly reorganized Trailways system. The name of the lines organized by M. E. Moore of Tennessee was changed to Continental Bus System on December 12, 1945. On September 5, 1946, all Bowen certificates were transferred by the ICC to Lone Star

A rare shot of the interior of a motor coach, Bowen Trailways #1274. ACF models typically contained a passenger seat up front with the driver, with the main door behind that passenger seat. The center aisle is about six inches lower than the rest of the bus floor, and signs on the seatbacks read Step Down to Aisle. *Motor Bus Society.*

Coaches, Inc., which changed its name to Continental Bus System on November 23, 1946.[25] All of this structure became the nucleus of M. E. Moore's Transcontinental Bus System, which received ICC approval December 9, 1947, and began corporate existence on Christmas Eve of 1947 with national headquarters in Dallas.[26]

As the Transcontinental Bus System, popularly known as Continental Trailways, expanded and developed from its Dallas offices, it symbolized in 1947 much of the history of Texas intercity bus transportation of the previous four decades. The new corporation, founded by a native of Tennessee and chartered in Delaware, nevertheless retained a deep sense of Texas heritage. It controlled Dutch Heket's Panhandle Stages. It owned and leased out a portion of Louis Hardy Creamer's Creamer

Stage Line from Eastland to San Antonio. It operated many of the original routes of Joe Amberson's Union Bus Lines. It incorporated within itself the Dixie-Sunshine network and the old Airline Motor Coaches. And of course it contained the immense bus empire of R. C. Bowen, who had now left the bus industry for the last time. Its routes stretched from deep East Texas to Denver, from El Paso to Texarkana, from the Rio Grande Valley to Houston and into New Mexico, Oklahoma, Arkansas, Louisiana, and, ultimately, almost all of the nation. It was a prosperous network as well. From July 1, 1942, through June 30, 1943, at the height of the war, Dixie-Sunshine alone transported 5,956,278 passengers.[27]

The Postwar Period

During that hectic period of wartime transportation, Dixie-Sunshine stretched its fleet of 175 buses to the limit, even resorting to school buses and tractor-trailer rigs to serve the needs of the military installations in Paris, Texarkana, Tyler, and Gainesville.[28] Bowen had used tractor-trailers extensively in Camp Bowie service from Dallas and Fort Worth, and Arrow briefly experimented with them from Waco to Brownwood. The buses were crowded, the terminals lively, and, despite the wartime restrictions, the bus lines were making a great deal of money. By mid-1944 it had become clearer to Americans, of course, that the United States would ultimately win the war, and the energies of America turned to planning for the postwar adjustment.

The first sign of adjustment for the bus industry came in the form of the removal of wartime restrictions. *Bus Transportation* was pleased to report such alleviations in July of 1945: "All restrictions on production and distribution of automotive replacement parts have been removed through a revision of Limitation Order L-158. WPB said that this action was taken in accord with recommendations for post-VE Day made by the Replacements Parts Industry Advisory Committee at its meeting on Aug. 24, 1944."[29] In the same issue, however, the journal had to acknowledge that the ODT orders remained in effect concerning production and delivery of intercity buses and that special permits still had to be obtained from ODT "before new intercity bus services may be

Demand for service to Camp Bowie was so great that Bowen pressed trailer buses into service during the war. This Dodge truck unit and driver were photographed at Camp Bowie during the height of wartime use, in July, 1942. Motor Bus Society.

started and before existing intercity bus services may be extended."[30]

The signs were there, however, that all restrictions would soon be lifted, and the bus industry joined the rest of the American people in looking forward with tremendous relief and optimism to the end of hostilities and a return to normal operations. The National Association of Motor Bus Operators was optimistic about the employment opportunities to be provided by the industry in the postwar recovery period: "Six thousand motor buses, representing an investment of $90 million, will be ordered by the nation's intercity bus lines as soon as the lifting of wartime priorities permits their manufacture. In addition, a program of rehabilitating all present equipment will provide employment for tens of thousands of automotive workers." Arthur M. Hill, president of NAMBO, continued the line of industry optimism in presenting the organizational survey of postwar needs in January of 1945: "Even when the pent-up demand is met, the anticipated postwar travel boom will send requirements for subsequent years above previous levels."[31] Several months later, however, in September of 1945, with World War II definitely over, Hill was more realistic in his message to the intercity bus industry. Pointing to "grave problems" ahead for the industry, he warned of "an inevitable decrease in revenues at war's end" and what he anticipated as "the greatly intensified competition for business we must expect from other forms of transportation."[32]

The form of transportation that would alter the bus industry the most was the passenger car. Wartime restrictions on production, tires, and fuel kept ownership and use of personal automobiles below normal demand levels. Now the troops were returning home, and life was adjusting to normal. Along with the baby boom would come the desire to spend more time with the family, to travel together, to make the pleasure and sightseeing trips that had not been possible during the war. And the postwar public, traveling together and for pleasure, most certainly did not wish to travel by bus. President Hill predicted and warned of this natural aversion to postwar intercity bus travel: "Wartime conditions of travel have undoubtedly impaired our public relations. This has been unavoidable, but nevertheless true. We have been compelled by circumstances to discourage bus travel, to permit crowding in buses, to render service which has been below standard as to scheduled efficiency and comfort."[33] Hill could also have mentioned the frequent breakdowns, the crowded terminals, the detours and temporary roadways that the buses were often forced to use, and the lengthy disruptions in scheduled services. All of these exigencies encountered during the war would cause fundamental problems for the intercity bus industry in its attempt to return to normal.

But for the most part the operators were optimistic. They believed that there would be so many aggregate postwar travelers that their segment of the transportation industry could prosper on just a fair share of the expanding market. A dominant theme in the postwar lit-

In anticipation of postwar prosperity bus companies wanted new designs, and manufacturers experimented with some. The Beck Company of Sidney, Ohio, designed this twin-level cruiser for Kerrville Bus Company, Inc., in the late 1940s. Kerrville Bus Company, Inc.

erature of the industry was improved public relations, another message stressed by Hill and the National Association of Motor Bus Owners.

Along with public relations went the theme of increased comfort and convenience. Hill had accurately understood the mood of the postwar public when he referred to the inconvenience and discomfort that the operators had to force on passengers during the war. An even more graphic account came from Guy J. Mann, who, along with L. R. Mabry, purchased Joe Amberson's Union Bus Lines in March of 1945. Mann was outspoken in his statement of what the public did not like about bus travel: "Furthermore, public comfort along the way is something that will need more attention from bus line operators.

Flxible delivered the two-thousandth of these popular postwar buses to T N M and O Coaches of Lubbock in 1947. The twenty-five-passenger, Chevrolet-powered bus is being conveyed to the T N M and O driver by Hugo Young, president of the Flxible Corporation. Motor Bus Society.

The public does not like to have to put up with the average run of makeshift accommodations found in the average juke-joint-honky-tonk way station, with their foul-smelling toilets, lack of towels, soap, or hot water. They feel entitled to at least railroad accommodations." Mann also felt that the operators would need to pay attention to advertising and public relations: "We intend to improve the public comfort along our right-of-way, and to start now to make our users bus-minded so that after the war they will think of bus travel first. . . . Most people use buses because they have no other alternative. We'd like to make it otherwise."[34] As a part of "making it otherwise" Mann recommended that buses become streamlined and roomier, more comfortable, safer, and faster. In a further display of his confidence in the in-

New equipment and new terminals of the late forties showed postwar modernism. The Brenham station was brand new when this photograph was taken in 1946. Kerrville Bus Company, Inc.

dustry, Mann joined B. H. Majors and Robert W. Hancock in August of 1945 in a partnership that bought Texas Motor Coaches of Fort Worth for a reported $280,000.[35]

Despite the efforts of Hill, Mann, and others to improve travel conditions, nationwide bus travel had peaked during 1944 and was never to return to the heady levels of the war. There were, however, still some reasons for postwar optimism. New equipment was indeed roomier and more comfortable. The companies could now purchase rolling stock with profits generated during the war. Wartime profits had also erased the debts of several operators, who now saw an opportunity to expand service. The nation turned its attention to rebuilding some of the secondary highways that the buses used. Several major railroads seemed markedly disinclined to compete for the passenger business, thus leaving a pool of potential customers for the bus industry.

Symbolic of the pent-up demand for vehicles during the war years, this fleet of six postwar T N M and O buses prepares to leave Ohio for the long "deadhead" drive back to home base in Lubbock. Number 812, the two-thousandth postwar Clipper, is second from the right in the lineup. Motor Bus Society.

Texas provided a microcosm of the national intercity bus industry in the attitude of its operators after the war. Not only were Mann and Mabry and the others planning to improve the "bus-mindedness" of the public, but most lines were expansionistic and hurried to purchase new equipment. Several operators who had intended to liquidate before 1941 had stayed in the bus business until the war was over and were now more than eager to sell out to younger managers. In addition to the expansion of Arrow Coach Lines, Dixie-Sunshine, and the Bowen concern, there were many other companies that maneuvered for market position as the war ended. Sue and W. L. Murphey purchased the Abilene–View–Robert Lee–San Angelo route from Robert McKissick, doing business as Abilene–San Angelo Coaches, on December 6, 1946.[36] The Kerrville Bus Company acquired from B. G. Creamer

Bus #1633, built by the American Car Foundry of Philadelphia, is ready for delivery to Texas Motorcoaches in Fort Worth on August, 29, 1940. Air-conditioning had already become a popular feature in the Texas market. Motor Bus Society.

the "alternate day" service certificate between San Angelo and San Antonio on July 9, 1945.[37] In September of 1947 Kerrville purchased the Bandera–Pipecreek–San Antonio service of L. L. Cook and James Amberson for a reported $40,000.[38] New terminals were being opened, new highways were being provided, and even a few new bus lines were initiating service, such as Chisholm Trail Stages from Stephenville to Vernon.

Probably the most prominent of the newcomers derived its existence from the inability and unwillingness of the railroads to attract a sufficient number of passengers in Texas after World War II. The Texas Electric Railway had been formed on January 1, 1917, by the merger of the Texas Traction Company and the Southern Traction Company.[39] The Texas Electric had a long and color-

Painter Bus Lines was a survivor in the postwar period of declining revenues. This 1948 coach is a twenty-nine-passenger bus with a Buick engine. Motor Bus Society.

ful history and could trace its origins to the charter of the Denison and Sherman Railway Company in 1900 and the departure of the first interurban from Denison on May 1, 1901. But the postwar years were not kind to the Texas Electric Railway. Its interurban base had shifted to Dallas-Waxahachie-Hillsboro-Waco before the war, and the upkeep of the long interurban line became cost prohibitive. The Railroad Commission authorized the creation of Texas Electric Bus Lines on November 6, 1948, to take over service from the aged and dilapidated interurban cars.[40] Texas Electric immediately placed an order for twenty coaches with the Flxible Company of Ohio.

There was a great deal of symbolism in the transition. On January 1, 1949, Flxible Clippers of the Texas Electric Bus Lines took over the interurban service between Dallas and Waco.[41] The lightweight rail cars were retired, and the buses glided along on the new postwar highway. Even those who noted the passing of the interurbans as "the end of an era" might not have realized, however, how much historical irony lay in the simple transfer from rails to buses between Waco and Dallas, for Texas Electric Bus Lines was not formed as a subsidiary to augment a railroad's passenger business—as had been true of the subsidiary efforts fostered by the Cotton Belt, Santa Fe, Southern Pacific, and Missouri Pacific—but rather to replace that passenger business with a mode of travel once deemed to be the unworthy competition. An additional note of irony came from the fact that the buses were operating over a highway that had been made so convenient, so weatherproof, so rapid, and so relatively safe that it had in and of itself provided devastating competition to the public rail line running alongside it.

And indeed the highway, with all its attractions, ultimately provided too much competition for Texas Electric Bus Lines and its postwar colleagues. Even as the new service began, trouble loomed ahead for the bus business nationwide and statewide. From a peak of 958 million riders in 1944, intercity bus ridership had declined to 950 million in 1945 and had begun an irreversible downward spiral that has continued to the present.

In the postwar period, once the operators realized that the boom in Texas intercity travel was not going to materialize, there was a rather rapid decline in the number of companies doing business in the state. Those that could find a buyer sold out fast. The larger lines stayed; the smaller ones disappeared. Many unprofitable lines were simply abandoned. By the mid-fifties a considerable roster of casualties had accumulated. Atascosa Bus Lines (San Antonio–Charlotte–Jourdanton) had been sold at a sheriff's auction. Kemp Bus Line ceased operations on a few days' notice. Rocksprings Motor Coaches no longer plied between Rocksprings and Kerrville via Ingram and Mountain Home. Chisholm Trail Stages succumbed with new Flxibles that were hardly broken in. Mooney Motor Coaches suddenly abandoned all of its extensive East Texas operations and simply disappeared. Rainbow Coaches decided to quit between Wichita Falls and Brownwood and stopped operating without notice. Service became sporadic or was suspended on many rural

This small, twenty-one-passenger unit, #240, was just right for the postwar demands of Kemp Bus Line, whose major route lay from Stephenville north to Mineral Wells, Jacksboro, and Graham. Kemp ceased operations in 1957. Motor Bus Society.

lines. Kerrville suspended its service between Fredericksburg and Junction via Harper. All operations ceased from Brady to Paint Rock and Ballinger. The Toliver brothers called it quits between Hillsboro and Corsicana. Kerrville bought the rights from Capitol City Lines to operate between Austin and Llano but discontinued the route just a few years later. Camp Bowie had been abandoned by the government as surplus property in 1949 and its operations transferred to Fort Hood, and it was no longer possible to take a bus from Brownwood to Cisco—a distance of about fifty miles—without making two transfers and arriving about four hours after departure.

In the mid-fifties the indefatigable Joe C. Carrington hosted a series of "Old Timers Bus Breakfasts" held in conjunction with the statewide conventions of the Texas Motor Transportation Association. One of the best-

This stripped-down Flxible was built for Mooney Motor Coaches in 1940 according to company specifications and at a cost of $1,940. Mooney was a relatively small operator whose routes covered the back roads of northeast Texas. Motor Bus Society.

attended of these convened in Dallas on November 5, 1956. Nearly one hundred people appeared for the breakfast, although several were younger associates paying tribute to the old-time bus operators and representing modern firms such as B. F. Goodrich, Firestone, and the Phillips Petroleum Company. But many others in the group were indeed pioneers, those who could reflect on the hectic adventures of prewar Texas bus lines and who could recall the first days of regulation in 1927 and the inception of the Texas Bus Owners Association. These people included Brian Bell, who had worked with Carrington in the thirties and now represented the Railroad Commission, as well as Carrington's loyal secretary, Gladys M. Shearer. The group also included George Wellington Hyde of Central Texas Bus Lines, Alice Rober-

J. C. Carrington, secretary-manager of the Texas Bus Owners Association and the Texas Motor Transport Association, was elected from Austin to terms in the Texas House of Representatives, in 1940 and 1942. Gladys M. Shearer.

son Cofer of Arrow, Guy Griggs of the Kerrville Bus Company, and C. D. Thomas, the cofounder of Airline Motor Coaches.[42]

There were others who sent regrets but whose names evoked fond memories from those who attended that breakfast in 1956: Henry English of Airline; Sam Day of Bee Line Coaches, a charter member of TBOA; Ed Eckstrom of Greyhound; Moss Patterson of the Oklahoma

Guy Griggs, the first president and chairman of the board of the Kerrville Bus Company, Inc. Kerrville Bus Company, Inc.

Transportation Company. Wardell Creamer wrote to the group: "Due to prior commitments cannot attend. J. C. is in Temple, Barnie at Kerrville and Papa [L. H. Creamer] at Comanche. Be sure and let me know when this will be held next year as want to be there. Give my regards to all."[43]

The Old Timers Bus Breakfast arranged by Carrington was held again in 1957, 1958, and 1959, but was eventually discontinued. They briefly recalled another time and place. The era of rowdiness in the Texas intercity bus industry—when Buicks forced W. B. Chenoweth off the road, when Mark Marshall organized the Motor Transportation Division of the Railroad Commission, when Power and Peterson battled the low-water bridges and the Union Bus Company at the same time, when Ed Abbott and W. L. Murphey and the others drove their jitneys around the oil fields, when Joe C. Carrington organized meetings and Walter Painter told his popular stories around the office, when R. C. Bowen "wheeled and dealed"—that era of pioneer motorbus operators in Texas had already passed away.

5. The Bus Lines of Oklahoma

The development of the intercity bus industry in both Oklahoma and New Mexico roughly paralleled that in Texas. Although the two neighboring states were, of course, smaller, they shared with Texas the common problems of poor highways, competition among pioneer operators, struggles to organize the owners, the imposition of regulation, and the economic uncertainties caused by two world wars and a depression. Both states were affected by the large passenger increases of wartime travel, and both saw their postwar bus revenues fade. The single most important difference between the two bordering states lay in the type of bus travel principally encouraged in each: resort operators developed a good deal of the bus business in New Mexico by attracting tourists to the Old West; the focus of bus travel in Oklahoma remained the transportation of the population from the outlying areas into the principal trade centers of Tulsa and Oklahoma City.

The records of the bus business in Oklahoma prior to the organization of the Oklahoma Motor Bus and Truck Operators Association in February of 1924 are not in good condition. It appears, however, that one of the earliest operations in the state did not in fact directly involve the larger population centers at all but was centered in the north-central city of Enid. An organization known as the Red Ball Bus and Baggage Company began carrying both freight and passengers from Enid to such communities as Watonga, Woodward, Canton, Kingfisher, Guthrie, and ultimately into Oklahoma City itself, in 1916.[1]

This Oklahoma Red Ball line appeared to have no connection with the Southland–Red Ball Bus Company operating in Texas in the 1920s, but it did prosper, as did the Texas line. By 1936, when its name had been changed to the Red Ball Bus Company, the Enid corporation had extended its routes considerably and had formed a rather large network with connections feeding into the route structures of Santa Fe Trail Stages and Southern Kansas Stage Lines. Operations in 1936 extended west to Liberal, Kansas, and east to Tonkawa. Setting aside the objections of the Rock Island Railroad and other potential competitors, the Interstate Commerce Commission on November 12, 1936, ordered that the Red Ball Bus Company have its franchise rights extended further to include through service between Woodward and Dodge City, Kansas.[2]

By the time of that 1936 ruling, the State Corporation Commission of Oklahoma had been in the business of awarding franchises for almost thirteen years. The commission began regulating the bus industry of the state in 1924, the same year in which the operators decided that they should organize to protect their interests. The Oklahoma Motor Bus and Truck Operators Association thus came into existence in February of 1924. The secretary-treasurer was R. G. Hickox of the Union Bus Station in Oklahoma City.[3]

From the beginning, the Oklahoma bus operators shared the general concerns of their Texas counterparts: stabilizing their route structures, ensuring freedom from wildcat competition, improving the highways, keeping costs low, and maximizing the return on their investments, all the while continuing to serve the traveling public. By the fifth annual convention, held in Muskogee on February 20 and 21, 1928, the bus owners were beginning to set an agenda quite similar to that to be developed by the Texas Bus Owners Association (which was to be organized and chartered within the next few weeks). The main concern of the companies represented at the 1928 convention was competition from illegal interstate operators. The group unanimously adopted a resolution urging the State Corporation Commission "to bar out interstate operators refusing to comply with the state laws relating to insurance, drivers' permits, and payment of mileage tax."[4]

By the time of the sixth annual convention, held in Oklahoma City on January 22 and 23, 1929, the attention of the membership had turned primarily toward the taxes that the Oklahoma legislature was proposing to levy on the bus industry. From a standard tax of one-fifth cent per mile per bus operated, the new legislation proposed a graduated scale, which would charge two cents per mile for full-sized buses and correspondingly smaller amounts for smaller vehicles. The bus owners were vigorously opposed to this change. Ward Faulkner of Ward Way Coaches in Muskogee admitted, however, that some small additional tax might well be levied so that the State Corporation Commission would have a source of revenue with which to "take vigorous action against illegal competition."[5]

Officers elected at the 1929 convention included most of the men then prominent in the bus business in Oklahoma. Carl Giles, a Norman operator, became president, with R. R. McCoy of Oklahoma City elected first vice-president. Second vice-president was J. Will Spurgin of Tulsa, owner of an outfit called Black and White Lines and just recently part of a merger to create M K and O Lines. Charles Mehew of Enid's Red Ball Bus and Baggage Company was elected third vice-president. R. G. Hickox, chairman of the association's legislative committee, continued as secretary-treasurer. The two additional directors were Ward Faulkner of Ward Way and Edgar Ross, a small operator from Vian in eastern Oklahoma.[6]

Moss Patterson's name was absent from this roster of dignitaries, but he was soon to become the leader of the organization and to direct the fortunes of one of the two largest bus companies in the state. He was born in Cainsville, Missouri, on July 20, 1893, but his parents soon moved to the Indian Territory, where Patterson grew up and completed high school near McCurtin. He eventually left the farm and began to sell Ford automobiles. He sold his thriving Ford dealerships to purchase one-half interest in the Oklahoma Transportation Company, a newly formed Oklahoma City concern, in 1929, and immediately became president and general manager of the bus company.[7]

Patterson's rise in the hierarchy of the Oklahoma bus business was swift. In November of 1929 he was elected president of the Oklahoma City Bus Terminal Association, composed of all of the bus owners using the Okla-

Howard Wesley Allen, the founder of M K and O Lines, poses beside one of his Reo coaches in Wichita, Kansas, about 1925. Allen began his first operations in the Wichita area in 1918 at the age of seventeen. M K and O Lines.

homa City Union Bus Terminal. Patterson's partner, Tom Cooper, was elected to the Board of Directors, as were Charles Mehew and Ward Faulkner. Another representative of the new M K and O Lines, E. A. Nash, was elected secretary-treasurer of the terminal association.[8]

By 1930 Patterson had been in the bus business only a few months but was nevertheless elected president of the Oklahoma Bus and Truck Association, succeeding Carl Giles, at the association's seventh annual convention, held February 12, 1930, in Tulsa. Other officers elected at this convention were familiar faces in the association: J. Will Spurgin of Tulsa became first vice-president; second vice-president was Charles E. Mehew of the Red Ball lines of Enid; R. G. Hickox continued as secretary-treasurer; Carl Giles and Ward Faulkner were the other directors.[9]

Primary concerns of this particular business meeting included a discussion of the fairest rate for bus lines to charge newspapers for hauling the papers to subscribers and distributors, but the standard issues of taxation, road conditions, and illegal operators also surfaced at the meet-

This makeshift motor coach was built for Allen's Auto Stage Line by the Wichita Carriage Works of M. A. McKenzie. Allen used McKenzie's vehicles — essentially a truck chassis with seats — until the delivery of his first Reo Speedwagon in 1924. M K and O Lines.

ing.[10] Special guests were A. T. Barrett, vice-president of TBOA, and Joe C. Carrington, TBOA secretary. In the course of the meeting, Carrington offered the interesting statistic that Texas bus owners were spending approximately $200,000 a year for local newspaper advertising. Carrington and Barrett assured the Oklahoma operators that the Texas Bus Owners Association, of which Moss Patterson was soon to become a director, shared the concerns of the Oklahoma operators and pledged the support of the TBOA in achieving the goals of the owners in both states.

In both Texas and Oklahoma, however, the organizations founded by bus operators followed similar paths and soon merged with trucking interests, although in Okla-

These Reo buses were extensively used by M K and O from 1925 to 1928, the probable time frame for this photograph taken in Oklahoma City. M K and O Lines.

homa the busmen enjoyed more organizational power after the merger than did their counterparts in Texas. At the February, 1931, meetings bus and truck owners pooled their interests to form a new association to be known as Motor Carriers of Oklahoma. The dominance of the bus people—which proved temporary—was reflected in the original roster of officers. Moss Patterson was the new president, and the directors included J. Will Spurgin and Charles E. Mehew, as well as M K and O executive Grover C. Jacobson. At the same time, however, the terms of the new organization stipulated that each of the groups of "A" and "B" truck operators should be entitled to one vice-president/director, and B. H. Clanton of Altus and R. A. Weicker of Oklahoma City were elected to those posts.[11] By the mid-thirties the associa-

This 1928 view of the M K and O Lines staff at the Cushing garage shows evidence of winter in Oklahoma. Howard Wesley Allen is in the dark suit and tie, wearing the topcoat. M K and O Lines.

tion known as Motor Carriers of Oklahoma had become primarily an organization advocating advantageous laws and court rulings for truckers.

Moss Patterson, meanwhile, continued to build the Oklahoma Transportation Company into the major route system in Oklahoma. So strong was the company during the thirties and into the war years that, along with M K and O Lines of Tulsa, it dominated highway transportation in the state and proved strong enough to thwart all takeover attempts by Southwestern Greyhound and other carriers. Patterson proved to be a shrewd administrator and pioneered the development of clean stations and bus stops. He did away with most "cash fares," prevalent on rural routes at the time, by establishing a larger-than-usual number of agents along his routes. Drivers would explain to cash customers that they could take

M K and O Lines coaches #64 and #62 are pictured with an Oklahoma A&M geology class on a field trip in the Arbuckle Mountains, in 1925 or 1926. M K and O Lines.

a cash fare only as far as the next agent, at which time the passenger would have to purchase a ticket to any other destination. Patterson also believed in a wide variety of concessions in his depots as another method of serving the public while recouping part of the cost of terminal upkeep.[12]

Under Patterson's management, the Oklahoma Transportation Company prospered and grew. The company reported that in 1928 it carried 159,988 revenue passengers. For 1929 the figure more than doubled, for a total of 360,181.[13] By the spring of 1930, the Oklahoma City Union Bus Terminal had fifty-eight daily departures, of which twenty were operated by the Oklahoma Transportation Company.

A less fortunate series of developments, however, befell Ward Faulkner's Ward Way Transportation Company, which at one time rivaled both Oklahoma Transportation and M K and O Lines for dominance of the route structure in eastern Oklahoma. Ward Way Transporta-

The M K and O Lines annual dinner, 1939 or 1940, at the Hotel Tulsa. Howard Allen's partner, J. Will Spurgin, is at the far right in the second row. John M. Allen.

tion buses traveled as far west as Oklahoma City, but the primary focus of the company was eastern Oklahoma, with company headquarters in Muskogee. In 1929 Ward Way reported that the 112 buses in its fleet had operated 3.5 million passenger miles over 1,300 miles of route system. In early 1930, the company estimated itself to be carrying forty thousand passengers a month and that three-fourths of that number would ultimately funnel through the new terminal facilities in Muskogee.[14] Company president Ward Faulkner, an influential member of the Oklahoma operators' association, even presented bonus checks to Ward Way employees who became parents of new children while on the company payroll.

By the autumn of 1930, however, the entire Ward Way system was in receivership. On October 27, 1930, federal judge R. L. Williams named McAlester fuel dealer J. G. Puterbaugh as Ward Way's receiver. By this time, Dean M.

Various makes and models of equipment used in 1929 by the expanding M K and O Lines are pictured: bus #11 (far right) is a Reo, the next is a Studebaker, #45 and the next two to the left are Reo vehicles, and the bus closest to the building and stairway is a White model 54. M K and O Lines.

Faulkner had taken over as president from his father. The creditors' suit that brought about the receivership action noted that expensive maturing obligations such as Ward Way's new Muskogee terminal could not be met.[15]

Despite this dramatic evidence of the effect of the Great Depression on the Oklahoma intercity bus business, Moss Patterson and others went forward with expansion plans during the thirties. The Red Ball Bus Company acquired the rights into Dodge City from Woodward in 1936 and then purchased the lines from Enid west to Pampa, Texas, from Dutch Heket's Panhandle Stage Lines in 1938.[16] B. D. Jordan expanded his Jordan Bus Company operations, originally begun in 1922, from his corporate base in Hugo, assumed much of the route structure of the Ward Way System, and developed an important network of service in southeastern Oklahoma.

In the late 1920s, before modernization, bus stations were frequently like this one at the northeast corner of Fourth and Cincinnati in Tulsa: a parking lot next to a hotel. An Art Deco bus terminal was later constructed on this site. M K and O Lines.

Moss Patterson and his partner Tom Cooper continued to develop connections with the Mid Continent Coaches and Rainbow Coaches operations to provide coordinated service from Oklahoma City to Chickasha, Duncan, Lawton–Fort Sill, Anadarko, Altus, Wichita Falls, Abilene, and Brownwood.[17] And some of the Ward Way operation gradually was subsumed into the operating territory of Oklahoma's other most important company, M K and O Lines.

M K and O Lines had its start not in Oklahoma but in Kansas, when in 1918 Howard Wesley Allen entered the bus business at the age of seventeen. Allen was so young that, according to a lifetime friend, his father had to sign bank notes for him to begin his local bus service around Wichita. Allen soon began operating his buses from Wichita to El Dorado and thus into the lucrative

M K and O Lines produced this sleek, full-color poster in the late 1930s, drawing favorable comment within the bus industry. The scene is on U.S. 66 at Devil's Elbow near Waynesville, Missouri. John M. Allen/M K and O Lines.

oil fields, and in 1923 he opened further service between Wichita and Newton. The fare charged between El Dorado and Wichita was fifty cents one way or ninety cents for a round-trip ticket.[18]

Allen's first bus consisted of a coach body welded to the chassis of two old cars. In due course, he was able to purchase equipment from Reo Speedwagon with the profits from his Wichita operations, and in 1925 he decided to move his entire venture to Cushing, Oklahoma. Beginning with a pair of Reo Speedwagons and a Hudson touring car, Allen established a highly successful bus line between Cushing and Tulsa in 1925 and christened the line Allen's Motor Lines. He soon added routes from Stillwater to Guthrie and Guthrie to Oklahoma City. Many of the highways were unpaved and constantly treacherous. When Allen began operating from Cushing to Tulsa, for example, the fifty-eight-mile route contained only about fifteen miles of pavement.[19]

The company known as M K and O Lines came into existence on September 29, 1928, when the State of Oklahoma issued a certificate of incorporation to Missouri, Kansas, and Oklahoma Coach Lines, Inc.[20] Corporate headquarters were listed as Tulsa. The partners in the

M K and O Lines briefly affiliated with the Trailways System in the late 1930s, and during this period the Tulsa shop rebuilt and repainted M K and O Trailways #57, an unusual combination of a Yellow Coach chassis and a Bender body. M K and O Lines.

$200,000 capital venture were J. Will Spurgin, Howard W. Allen, A. S. (Mrs. J. Will) Spurgin, and M. L. (Mrs. Howard W.) Allen, all of Tulsa. M K and O Lines was an amalgamation of Spurgin's services and Allen's Stage Lines and immediately controlled the bus territory of northeastern and north central Oklahoma.

Will Spurgin's Black and White Lines included routes from Tulsa to Coffeyville and service from Tulsa to the nearby towns of Jenks, Bixby, and Broken Arrow. Allen's Motor Lines extended west via Sapulpa, Drumright, Oilton, and Cushing to Guthrie, Edmond, and Oklahoma City. Service to Vinita soon followed, and the prewar era saw M K and O service extended to Joplin, Springfield, and ultimately St. Louis.

As the route structure of M K and O expanded, so did its fleet. A report to the Interstate Commerce Commis-

Veteran driver Tom Amick started with Allen's Auto Stage in 1919 at the age of fourteen. This photograph was taken in 1925. Tom Amick.

sion at the close of 1938 showed twenty-seven vehicles on the service roster of the line. The most recent acquisitions listed in the report were a Yellow Coach thirty-six-passenger model purchased in January of 1938 and three Flxible buses delivered in November.[21] Throughout World War II, of course, the pace of delivery and acquisition slowed down, and M K and O Lines was able to purchase just nine new buses from 1941 to 1945.[22]

By the mid-thirties the M K and O Lines structure was stabilizing, business was good between Tulsa and Oklahoma City, and ridership had increased from 166,000 in 1929 to over 500,000 in 1936.[23] At this juncture Allen decided to experiment with the fledgling Trailways network and brought M K and O into the Trailways system in 1936. The relationship was to last only a few years, and M K and O always retained its separate corporate identity, although there were some temporary advantages for both Trailways and M K and O in terms of schedules and connections.

In the late thirties M K and O Trailways purchased a series of twenty-nine-passenger White buses and rebuilt

Pinky Carson began driving for Howard W. Allen in 1938 at the age of twenty and finally retired from M K and O in 1982. In the winter of 1941 he was photographed in Tulsa in full driver's regalia next to M K and O #303. William P. Carson.

them in the Tulsa shop into coaches with a more streamlined appearance. Longtime employees of M K and O Lines still can recall the considerable activity around the shop in the late thirties and early forties, as M K and O raided the salvage yards to locate suitable spare parts. All can remember the conversion of the Whites and the transfer of company allegiance to General Motors and Flxible products around 1940.[24]

World War II had its anticipated effect on the intercity bus lines of Oklahoma. Just as in Texas and the rest of the country, the operators had serious difficulty getting parts, mechanics, and new buses. So serious were the maintenance problems on M K and O Lines that one Springfield–St. Louis schedule had a record-breaking eight flat tires in the course of a single trip. A veteran driver had to abandon a bus that was in regular service

Santa Fe Trail Stages was an important link in the network of bus lines stretching from Chicago to Los Angeles. It ultimately connected with M K and O operations in Tulsa and Wichita and became a vital part of the Trailways route structure. Tom Amick.

in Springfield in 1943 because exhaust fumes had leaked into the coach, and there were simply no mechanics to work on the problem. The stranded passengers had to wait for the next schedule. As late as the beginning of the war, there were still many segments of the route that were unpaved. Those that particularly irritated the drivers and the public were the gravel stretches from Stillwater to Oilton and from Mount Vernon to Republic in Missouri.[25]

From the beginning Howard Wesley Allen was the driving force behind M K and O Lines, and at the outset of the war he bought out the Spurgin interests and assumed full control of the corporation. Allen prided himself on saying that he had personally ridden buses over every foot of the line. His employees developed a tenacious loyalty to him, many of them making lifetime careers of their

These eighteen-passenger, Chevrolet-powered Flxibles, #135, #134, and #133, were delivered to the Oklahoma Transportation Company in 1941. Motor Bus Society.

jobs at M K and O. Reports of employee enthusiasm for the company and its leader appeared in several industry publications, including *Riding the Trails with Trailways:*

> Its [M K and O] advancement was not made by just better times but by giving the public something better, something they were not expecting, and that was Good Bus Service. Large luxurious motor coaches, frequent convenient schedules, well-trained employees, courteous, polite, and ever alert to their duties—All of this has been accomplished under the guiding hand of Mr. H. W. Allen, President and General Manager of the M K and O. Mr. Allen has placed motor transportation to this new level of popularity.[26]

Although Howard Allen kept his bus business totally within the family, Tom Cooper decided that the end of the war was a good time to sell out his interests in the Oklahoma Transportation Company. Cooper had bought out Moss Patterson in the late thirties, and Patterson,

These models were the "top of the line" when Oklahoma Transportation took delivery in 1941 and proudly proclaimed that they were air-conditioned. Motor Bus Society.

after extensive war service, returned to the bus business as president of Mid-Continent Trailways. Mid-Continent had earlier integrated its routes with Southwest Coaches and Rainbow Coaches to serve a vast territory from Garden City to Oklahoma City and from Wichita to Abilene and had also subsumed the Red Ball Bus Company. By war's end Cooper was more than ready to cease his connections with the bus industry. He found a willing buyer in Eugene Jordan of Jordan Bus Company. When the Oklahoma Transportation Company changed hands in the summer of 1945, it was purchased from Cooper for two million dollars. The buyers were Eugene Jordan and his wife, Julia, along with Robert S. Bowers, Tom Cooper's son-in-law, who became president of the company. Jordan and his partners also purchased the Oklahoma Railway Company, the municipal transportation system of Oklahoma City, at this time. As of July, 1945,

Southwestern Greyhound Lines was also a major presence in Oklahoma and did a large volume of business on its routes from Tulsa to Dallas. Number 207, a thirty-seven-passenger model developed by the General American Aerocoach Company of East Chicago, Indiana, was delivered in 1941. Motor Bus Society.

Oklahoma Transportation operations covered one thousand highway miles, with principal routes extending from Oklahoma City to Fort Smith, Ardmore, and Wichita Falls.[27]

The same postwar experience that befell Texas, however, soon overtook the bus industry in Oklahoma. M K and O expanded its route structure in 1945 to include service from Tulsa to Enid via Perry. The Oklahoma lines rejoiced in the ability to buy new parts and rolling stock. DOT cars with gasoline motors were delivered to M K and O in 1946.[28] And the intercity companies hurried to procure new vehicles to service the anticipated travel boom.

But there was to be no such boom. In Oklahoma, as

in Texas, the heyday of the bus business was over. The principal traffic in Oklahoma had been composed of three groups: the military, those just passing through, and rural passengers. But the end of the war slowed down the volume of traffic at Fort Sill and Tinker Air Force Base, and the Great Depression had previously emptied the farms and small agricultural communities of their population. The through passengers might buy a sandwich in the Oklahoma City terminal but, unless traveling on the main line connections of M K and O or Oklahoma Transportation, contributed little revenue to smaller rural lines such as Jordan. Bus service in the state quickly gravitated toward the two major independents, Mid-Continent Trailways, or the through services offered by Greyhound in conjunction with M K and O (Los Angeles–Chicago via Tulsa and St. Louis) or by Trailways in conjunction with Oklahoma Transportation (Wichita-Dallas via Oklahoma City and Ardmore). Howard Allen brought his son Robert into the business, diverted his attention to ranching and livestock, and then continued more or less to preside over the gradual decline of the Oklahoma bus business until his death in an airplane accident in 1964.[29] His death brought an end to the era of pioneer motorbus operators in Oklahoma.

6. The Bus Lines of New Mexico

The intercity bus industry developed in a slightly different manner in New Mexico because of the sustained importance of tourism in that state. Whereas the Texas and Oklahoma bus operators concerned themselves mainly with the transportation of passengers who needed to get somewhere, a significant portion of the bus industry in New Mexico grew up around the concept that tourists from other parts of the country would pay to have their progress through New Mexico smoothed.

Such was the premise of Maj. R. Hunter Clarkson of Scotland, who became affiliated during the early twenties with the Fred Harvey organization and thus with the Passenger Traffic Division of the Atchison Topeka and Santa Fe Railway. Hunter Clarkson envisioned the potential in having tourists leave the main line of the Santa Fe for excursions into the Indian country of northern New Mexico. He hoped to accomplish these "Indian detours" by using elegant touring cars designed so that the "dudes" could get the maximum view of the landscape and its inhabitants.

Since Clarkson realized that he did not have the capital to underwrite this venture, he took the idea to Ford Harvey, the son of the late Fred Harvey and the head of the Harvey organization. The plan seemed reasonable for a Harvey venture because Harvey already owned hotels at Las Vegas, Albuquerque, and Santa Fe and could easily handle the business that Clarkson's proposal might generate.[1] After several weeks of planning and scouting, Clarkson and W. J. Black, passenger traffic manager for the Santa Fe, made joint announcements in Albuquerque and Chicago that Indian Detours would begin operations in time for the spring and summer travel season of 1926.[2]

Clarkson was the featured speaker at a dinner in the

This vehicle, manufactured by White for Indian Detours and known as a "Harveycar," is waiting for the rest of its passengers before departing from Santa Fe in 1926. Motor Bus Society.

La Fonda Hotel of Santa Fe on August 29, 1925. He explained the idea to members of the Santa Fe Chamber of Commerce and a number of other dignitaries from around the state. He labeled the detour as a "three-day, three hundred-mile motor tour to be furnished Santa Fe railroad tourists on an all-expense, bother-eliminated basis."[3] The plan was for eastbound tourists to leave the train at Albuquerque, tour that area and then Santa Fe, and reboard the eastbound train three days later at Las Vegas. Westbound passengers would leave the train at Las Vegas and resume their trips at Albuquerque in three days. Santa Fe and its environs were to be the focus of the trip, and all passengers would be boarded exclusively

At Tesuque Pueblo in 1926 Harveycar passengers converse with Indian shopkeepers while the driver and tour guide take a break. Motor Bus Society.

at Fred Harvey establishments in the three communities. The Castañeda Hotel would serve as the base camp in Las Vegas, with the La Fonda the focal point of the Santa Fe experience and the Alvarado the rendezvous site in Albuquerque.

With the starting date tentatively set as May 15, 1926, Clarkson and his crew had no time to waste. Ford Harvey purchased the garage of the Thomas Motor Company in Santa Fe as an operational headquarters for Indian Detours at a rumored price of sixty thousand dollars, and the planners agreed on forty-five dollars as the price for the three-day, "bother-eliminated" tour.[4]

A major decision concerned the proper vehicles for the rather demanding terrain that the buses would have to travel. Two coaches were ordered from the Yellow Coach Company of Chicago to serve as test vehicles. Major Clarkson, Ford Harvey's son Frederick, J. E. Shirley

Along the Indian Detour in 1926, the "Detourists" visit with a native rider while the Harveycar is stopped along a gravel road. Motor Bus Society.

of the Fred Harvey Grand Canyon operation, and several other officials rode the Yellow coaches in a test run on Wednesday, December 16, 1925, between Las Vegas and Santa Fe. The group decided that the coaches would do and secured an agreement from the appropriate state officials for road improvements along the route.[5]

In addition to the Yellow coaches that would accommodate either sixteen or twenty-six passengers, Clarkson and Frederick Harvey ordered nineteen eleven-passenger coaches from the White Company of Cleveland. Both the White and Yellow buses featured swivel seats upholstered in leather and extra large windows so that all of the "Detourists" would get good views of the countryside. Nine seven-passenger Packard touring cars rounded out the fleet. All of the buses provided extra luggage facilities, because the railroad and its new affiliate guaranteed through-checking of all luggage on the Indian Detours

A Harveycar has made a noontime stop at the Apache Inn, Valley Ranch, New Mexico, and is just about to reload passengers to continue the Indian Detour. Motor Bus Society.

to allay the fears of passengers that their luggage might not be transferred from train to bus at Las Vegas or Albuquerque.[6]

Clarkson and Harvey decided to arrange a trial run for the public, and the preview caravan departed from the Alvarado Hotel in Albuquerque on Saturday morning, March 27, 1926, arriving on schedule at the Castañeda in Las Vegas on Monday evening the twenty-ninth. This preview used the same coaches over the same proposed route. No problems developed, and regular service commenced on the Indian Detours on May 15, 1926.[7]

The official operating organ of the Indian Detours was the Santa Fe Transportation Company, which was organized in Delaware on November 25, 1925, with a capital stock of $500,000. Byron S. Harvey was the president of this new corporation, which was formed not only to promote the detours but to provide supplemental service to the Santa Fe Railway schedules in New Mexico.[8] Soon the subsidiary was providing other bus service in addition to the Indian Detours.

A company known as New Mexico Motorways had been providing some bus service between Santa Fe and Albuquerque via Bernalillo, and the Santa Fe Transportation Company bought out New Mexico Motorways on September 21, 1926.[9] The company undertook to provide bus service for the sixteen-mile connection between Lamy and Santa Fe, whereupon the Santa Fe Railway could discontinue its unprofitable branch line train service between those points. Other regular routes were soon added from Santa Fe to Las Vegas and from Santa Fe to Raton via Taos. *Bus Transportation* reported the following equipment in use in January of 1927:

> Fifteen Model 53 Whites with 11-passenger bodies and swivel chairs, for Indian Detour service.
> Two Model 50-B Whites with 26-passenger bodies, for regular bus service between Lamy and Santa Fe.
> One Model "Y" Yellow with 26-passenger body.
> Three Model "X" Yellows with 17-passenger bodies. These Yellows are for regular bus service between Albuquerque and Santa Fe.
> Two Model 53 Whites with 26-passenger bodies, for regular bus service between Las Vegas and Santa Fe.
> Ten Packard Straight Eight, 7-passenger sedans and touring cars, for optional trips and motor land cruises.[10]

While the three-day tours continued to be operated as luxury cruises for the Detourists, the remaining routes of the Santa Fe Transportation Company served as conventional intercity bus routes. Trucks supplemented the buses plying their way between Santa Fe and Lamy to handle the large volume of baggage and express traffic connecting the state capital with the vital main line of the railroad. In 1927 the company operated one daily round-trip from Santa Fe to Las Vegas, "on demand" service to Taos and Raton, three daily round-trips between Santa Fe and Albuquerque, and six round-trips daily between Santa Fe and Lamy.[11]

Very soon after its inception, then, the Santa Fe Transportation Company had become a major force in the transportation patterns of New Mexico: "In 1927 the 48 units of equipment operated by the transportation company covered a total of 699,998 miles. Of this total 275,810 miles were covered by the Indian-detour motor coaches, 175,355 miles by the automobiles on special tours, and 123,453 miles by the motor coaches used on the three regular routes."[12] In 1928 there came a major schedule change: the eastern terminus for the Detourists became Lamy rather than Las Vegas; and after May 15, 1928, all those passengers taking the Indian Detours spent their nights in the La Fonda and the Alvarado.[13]

In 1929 the Ninth Legislature of the State of New Mexico created a Motor Transportation Department within the State Corporation Commission for the purpose of protecting the public interest in matters pertaining to the conveyance of passengers and freight for hire. Certificates were to be issued to appropriate and legitimate carriers of record under the stipulations known as Chapter 129. The law provided that all carriers had ninety days from March 12, 1929, in which to comply with the new directives. The Santa Fe Transportation Company of Delaware was predictably successful in demonstrating the reliability and longevity of its service and obtained six operating certificates from the Motor Transportation Department on September 30, 1929, authorizing service from Santa Fe to Lamy, Taos, Las Vegas, Albuquerque, and over the Detours.[14]

As in Texas and Oklahoma, the formation of a regulatory agency precipitated efforts to found an association to protect the interests of the bus owners. Fifteen busmen from around the state gathered in Santa Fe in March of 1929 and formed the New Mexico Truck and Bus Owners' Association. Charles Hill of Las Cruces was elected president; Guy Wallace of Albuquerque, vice-president; and P. A. Steffan of Roswell, secretary-treasurer. Fred Parrish of Silver City, owner of the Parrish Stage Line between his hometown and El Paso, was a principal organizer and director. The meeting declared the purpose of the group to be "to promote the interests of its members, and to improve both passenger and freight service on motor lines in this state."[15]

Despite the enthusiastic reviews from contented tourists and the stories on the company's successes in *Railway Age* and *Bus Transportation*, however, the Indian Detours never turned a profit. They contributed heavily to the revenues of the Fred Harvey hotels, restaurants, and gift shops, but the lines themselves were costly to operate. Equipment wore out on the difficult terrain; couriers and drivers had to be specially trained to handle the needs of the Detourists; each vehicle had to be maintained with the greatest care so that railroad standards of elegance could be provided on the luxury land cruiser; and, of course, every resource had to be constantly expended in the effort to guarantee connections with the railroad. Annual operating losses ranged from a low of $29,630.30 in 1929 to a rather formidable $65,539.73 in 1930. Ford Harvey died in 1928, and his brother Byron became president of the Harvey organization. With losses averaging over $9,000 a month in January and February of 1931, Byron Harvey decided to sell the Indian Detours and to concentrate his efforts on bus tours at the Grand Canyon.[16]

The new owner was R. Hunter Clarkson, who immediately formed a corporation known simply as Hunter Clarkson, Inc., to take over the assets of the line. Clarkson assumed control on March 1, 1931.[17] There were to be no major disruptions of service on the line throughout the Depression. Clarkson continued to cooperate in every way with the Santa Fe, and most passengers were probably unaware that the Indian Detours had changed hands. As the Depression and World War II proceeded, however, there was an inevitable decline in the number

This conveyance is poised to meet the Santa Fe train at Lamy in 1938. Note the porthole windows on this Kenworth model. Motor Bus Society.

of tourists interested in the Detours and, in fact, the Office of Defense Transportation declared the three-day tours "non-essential" in 1942 and suspended them for the duration of the war, although the regular bus routes were allowed to operate from Santa Fe.

By this time the Indian Detours themselves had undergone a change. Clarkson limited the focus of the operation to Lamy–Santa Fe and to the tours radiating from Santa Fe. Albuquerque–Santa Fe local service became the province of Frank McCutchen's Inter City Transit Lines, while both the Greyhound and Trailways networks traveled the roads in regular service between Raton, Las Vegas, Santa Fe, and Albuquerque.

Other operators, meanwhile, were busy in New Mexico. Fred Parrish kept developing his El Paso–Las Cruces–Silver City business. Grover McMakin extended the routes of McMakin Motor Coaches westward from Lub-

This sixteen-passenger coach was delivered to Inter City Transit Lines on December 9, 1935, by the Superior Coach Company. Despite the list of cities on the side of the coach, ICTL never served El Paso or Farmington. Motor Bus Society.

bock into Roswell, Hobbs, and Carlsbad. H. T. Page developed the Page-Way System from Las Vegas to Carlsbad and south to Pecos, Texas, for connections with Kerrville and Greyhound. The man who achieved the most enduring success in the New Mexico intercity bus business, however, was a native of Oklahoma named Paul McCutchen.

McCutchen moved to Roswell as a young man in 1910 and worked at various jobs in that city until 1918, when he became a driver for Carl McNally of the White Line Stage Company. The White Line had begun operations during World War I between Roswell and Carrizozo, and it was this route that McCutchen drove. McNally wanted to extend a line north to Vaughn but did not have the equipment or capital and took McCutchen in as a partner. Soon McCutchen had developed a service connect-

One of the most prominent men in the New Mexico bus business, Paul McCutchen began his career as a driver for the White Line in 1918. He is here pictured in Roswell beside his Roswell-Alamogordo Stage. New Mexico Transportation Company.

ing Roswell and Alamogordo. Other routes quickly followed so that his New Mexico Transportation Company (NMTC) buses were serving Roswell from Santa Fe, Clovis, and Albuquerque.[18] After a stint with the company as traffic manager, Paul's brother Frank moved to Albuquerque, where he began the Inter City Transit Lines after purchasing the Santa Fe–Albuquerque rights from Hunter Clarkson.[19]

Paul McCutchen was also active in the operators' association and was elected a director of the Motor Carriers Association of New Mexico at its 1930 meeting.[20] But his primary interest seemed to lie in expanding his bus company. With the anticipated establishment of the Interstate Commerce Commission in 1935, McCutchen moved to consolidate his route structure and incorporated the New Mexico Transportation Company, Inc., in January of 1935, with Roswell as corporate headquarters.[21]

Appropriate certificates of public convenience and necessity were issued to the New Mexico Transportation Company on September 17 and December 7, 1935, for intrastate operation between Alamogordo and Vaughn,

One of the oldest bus companies in New Mexico, the White Line operated between Roswell and Carrizozo during World War I. Owner Carl McNally was in the trucking business in Roswell. The young woman pictured is thought to be his daughter. Pat Fuqua.

Clovis and Tucumcari, and Willard and Mountainair.[22] In 1937, however, Paul McCutchen filed to make these particular certificates interstate in nature and to reaffirm his rights to service between Roswell and the major cities of El Paso, Amarillo, Albuquerque, and Santa Fe.

A long and bitter set of hearings emanated from that initial submission on February 3, 1937. The Santa Fe Railway, the Southern Pacific Company, and Hunter Clarkson, Inc., intervened for the purpose of protecting their interests. The commission ruled on April 28, 1937, that the New Mexico Transportation Company was entitled to all of the rights and privileges that it had sought except for a lone concession to Hunter Clarkson: "Said certificate shall be restricted so as not to authorize applicant to transport interstate passengers between Santa Fe and Lamy, picked up at either of these points, except when destined beyond Santa Fe and Lamy over lines of

Cadets from the New Mexico Military Institute at Roswell scamper on the dunes on a 1938 outing to White Sands National Monument. Pat Fuqua.

applicant or those of connecting carriers with which it has specific interchange arrangements."[23] The most important interchange arrangements for McCutchen were with Southwestern Greyhound Lines, and in 1938 the two companies formed a "through-ticket" agreement that lasted throughout the postwar period. Passengers could now be "routed through the Land of Enchantment" by Greyhound agents from Amarillo to El Paso with a permissible stop at Carlsbad Caverns National Park.[24]

On June 27, 1941, New Mexico Transportation Company received ICC permission to purchase, for thirty thousand dollars, all of the operating rights of H. T. Page's Page-Way Stage Lines, Inc., operating between Las Vegas and Pecos, Texas, via Artesia and Carlsbad. In declaring the assets of his company at the time of the sale, Mc-

Note the half door on this White model, #27, for New Mexico Transportation Company. It is located about two-thirds of the way back on the panel lettered "Roswell" and is an emergency exit. Motor Bus Society.

Cutchen revealed that he owned 53 percent of New Mexico Transportation Company, his brother Frank owned 2 percent, and the remaining 45 percent was owned by Southwestern Greyhound Lines, Inc.[25]

After the excessive demands of World War II, the intercity bus industry in New Mexico settled down to prepare for the boom in travel that so many in the national bus industry had predicted. To some extent this boom's failure to materialize was felt less harshly in New Mexico than in Texas or Oklahoma because of the industry's dependence on tourism. Indian Detours had begun with the premise of serving passengers who had extra money and extra time, and because it had for the most part been declared nonessential in 1942 it had not become mired in the excesses of wartime travel. The detours had thus not become associated with the hardship and difficult travel of the rest of the bus industry in the minds of the

Flxible delivered this eighteen-passenger model to New Mexico Transportation Company in April of 1941. Note that this NMTC Clipper now carries the emblem of the Greyhound dog. Motor Bus Society.

passengers. The company still had a good reputation that hearkened back to the simpler prewar era.

A related factor was that New Mexico had never depended for the success of its intercity bus industry on local business. With the vast distances between villages, New Mexico had built a bus industry that was generally in it "for the long haul." That sort of operation tended to fare better in the postwar era than did the hamlet-to-county seat venture. It was no trouble to get into one's new car and drive ten miles to the county seat, after all; but it was worth a second thought when that county seat was one hundred miles away across the sand dunes.

The Santa Fe Railway reclaimed direct responsibility for the Indian Detours after the war, with Hunter Clarkson and the railroad dissolving the corporations that had been formed to guide the enterprise. The railroad took

When the Roswell terminal first opened its doors, on May 15, 1948, Paul McCutchen's bus lines were carrying 650,000 passengers annually. The corporate offices of New Mexico Transportation were on the second floor. New Mexico Transportation Company.

over the Detours again on December 23, 1947, and operated some form of the service until the Santa Fe passenger trains were absorbed into Amtrak. The name "Indian Detours" was purchased by Frank McCutchen, Jr.[26]

A convenient date for concluding this sketch of the New Mexico intercity bus industry is Saturday, May 15, 1948. On that date Paul McCutchen's New Mexico Transportation Company, Inc., opened its new state-of-the-art bus terminal in downtown Roswell. The occasion prompted the *Roswell Morning Dispatch* to note that the company operated 3.4 million miles annually, owned forty-two buses with more on order, employed ninety full-time workers, and carried 650,000 passengers every year. The newspaper stated that at least five NMTC buses were "on the road at every moment of the day or night."[27]

Paul W. Tibbetts, who had been a colleague of Joe Carrington's in the Texas Bus Owners Association and a TBOA director, attended the ceremonies in Roswell on May 15, 1948, as a vice-president of New Mexico Transportation. But Tibbetts' primary role at the ceremony was even more symbolic. In the intervening years he had become president of Southwestern Greyhound Lines, which at the time of the terminal opening controlled 45 percent of NMTC stock. A newspaper story stated that "Mr. Tibbetts, through his co-operation, has been of great assistance in the development of the company."[28] Within a few years, the New Mexico Transportation Company would become a wholly owned subsidiary of Greyhound Lines.

On May 15, 1948, however, the concerns of forced mergers and disappearing passenger loads, of increasing costs and declining revenues, were undoubtedly not on the minds of Paul McCutchen and his associates. They, like their counterparts in Texas and Oklahoma, stood ready to transfer the pioneer motorbus spirit to the postwar period. Their inventory rosters were growing, and their futures appeared bright. When the traveling public called, operators like Paul McCutchen in New Mexico, Howard W. Allen in Oklahoma, and Guy Griggs in Texas would surely be ready to play their parts.

Notes

Chapter One.
From the
Beginnings
to Regulation

1. Leonard G. Simon, "Texas' First Bus Run: 30 Miles in 12 Hours." See also Walter B. Moore, "Preachers Warned against First Texas Bus"; and "Texas Pioneers in Transportation"; "Truck Men to Honor Pioneer"; "Inventors to Honor Forgotten Man."

2. Leonard G. Simon, "The Start of America's Amazing Bus Industry," 1:131–32.

3. Ibid., p. 132.

4. Joe C. Carrington, former secretary-manager, Texas Bus Owners Association, Inc., interview, Austin, Tex., February 6, 1980.

5. Wendell O'Neal, *Motor Busses in Texas 1912–1930*, p. 59. This volume, privately printed for the Texas Bus Owners Association (TBOA), represented an effort by the association to strengthen its position and standing with bus operators of the day. O'Neal was at the time editor of the association's house journal, *Motor Transportation in Texas*. After describing a few of the conditions existing before regulation, O'Neal gives a rather detailed account of the inception of the Motor Transportation Division of the Railroad Commission and of the TBOA itself. A large part of the book is devoted to sketches of early Texas bus operators. These sketches resulted from O'Neal's questionnaire to the owners, however, and frequently need considerable independent verification. Nonmembers and nonrespondents are not included. Many of the respondents seemed to be more interested in providing nicknames and anecdotes about their families than in discussing the bus business. The book is nevertheless invaluable to those interested in this field. The very few surviving copies are primarily in collections, such as those of the Texas State Archives and the Barker Texas History Center at the University of Texas at Austin.

6. Oscar Schisgall, *The Greyhound Story: From Hibbing to Everywhere*, pp. 4, 6.

7. O'Neal, *Motor Busses in Texas*, p. 105.

8. Wayne E. Fuller, *RFD: The Changing Face of Rural America*, pp. 194–95, 197, 198.

9. O'Neal, *Motor Busses in Texas*, p. 78.
10. Ibid., pp. 78, 81.
11. Ibid., p. 113.
12. Alice Roberson Cofer, former owner, Arrow Coach Lines, interview, Lampasas, Tex., February 8, 1980.
13. W. L. Murphey, co-owner and president of Sun Set Stages, interview, Abilene, Tex., June 30, 1971. Also Bill R. Murphey, president; Mary Murphey, secretary-treasurer; Pat Murphey, vice-president; and Sue Murphey, wife of W. L. Murphey, all of Sun Set Stages, interviews, Abilene, Tex., January–February, 1980.
14. O. C. Murphey, "Report to the Motor Transportation Division." June, 1927, Sun Set Stages File, Railroad Commission of Texas files.
15. "G. W. Hyde: Success Story—Central Texas Bus Line," pp. 10, 11; G. W. Hyde, founder of Central Texas Bus Lines, interview, Cleburne, Tex., February 20, 1980.
16. O'Neal, *Motor Busses in Texas*, pp. 15, 18.
17. Ibid., p. 18.

Chapter Two.
The Era of
Regulation
and Organization

1. "An Act to Regulate Motor Propelled Passenger Vehicles Engaged Regularly in the Business of Transporting Passengers for Hire over the Public Highways of the State of Texas; Defining Motor Bus Companies and Declaring Them Common Carriers," chapter 270, General Laws of the Fortieth Legislature of the State of Texas, 1927 (hereafter, Motor Bus Law of 1927).
2. O'Neal, *Motor Busses in Texas*, p. 20.
3. Motor Bus Law of 1927, Section 4(a).
4. Ibid., Section 5.
5. Ibid.
6. Carrington interview.
7. Ibid.
8. O'Neal, *Motor Busses in Texas*, p. 20.
9. Mark Marshall, "Report of the Motor Transportation Division," December 31, 1927, Railroad Commission of Texas files.
10. Ibid. See also the discussion of this report in O'Neal, *Motor Busses in Texas*, pp. 20–24.
11. "We Mourn," pp. 3, 4.
12. "R. C. Bowen, Breckenridge, Texas," handwritten account in the files of the Motor Bus Society Library. For corroboration, see Earl F. Theisinger, "R. C. Bowen of Texas," p. 542.
13. Charter, Texas Bus Owners Association, Article 2, p. 1, March 24, 1928, my files.

14. Ibid., pp. 2–4.

15. Minutes of the First Meeting of the Board of Directors of the Texas Bus Owners Association, April 4, 1928, p. 1, my files.

16. Ibid., p. 2. Temporary funds of eighteen hundred dollars were subscribed toward the organization's expenses by those present.

17. Minutes, April 4, 1928, pp. 2–3.

18. Minutes of the Second Meeting of the Board of Directors of the Texas Bus Owners Association, April 13, 1928, p. 1, my files.

19. Ibid., p. 3.

20. Guy J. Shields to J. C. Carrington, April 20, 1928, my files; and Minutes, April 4, 1928, p. 2.

21. "Motor Bus Rules and Regulations Adopted by the Railroad Commission of Texas Effective June 1, 1928," 1930, p. 8 and passim, Railroad Commission of Texas files.

22. Minutes of the Third Meeting of the Directors of the Texas Bus Owners Association, May 25, 1928, p. 1, my files.

23. Ibid., passim.

24. J. C. Carrington, "Suggested Plan of Work for the TBOA," typed document prepared for meeting of May 25, 1928, my files.

25. Minutes, May 25, 1928, p. 2.

26. Code of Ethics of the Texas Bus Owners Association, Inc., adopted July 25, 1928, Dallas, Tex., as reprinted in O'Neal, *Motor Busses in Texas*, p. 43.

27. Ibid., Article 11.

28. Minutes, May 25, 1928, p. 4.

29. "Bus Chatter," September, 1930, p. 22.

30. *Motor Transportation in Texas* had a great deal to do with the dissemination of accurate information about the regulations of the Motor Transportation Division. The "Bus Chatter" section varied from half a column to three pages. It featured news of families, terminals, and current jokes making the rounds of the depots. Much of its space was devoted to permits issued by the Railroad Commission.

31. O'Neal, *Motor Busses in Texas*, pp. 40–41.

32. Carrington interview; Gladys McCarty Shearer, secretary to Joe C. Carrington, interviews, Austin, Tex., 1980–85. It is largely due to Ms. Shearer's efforts to preserve documents and correspondence that the material for this history survived.

33. Mark Marshall, "Report of the Motor Transportation Division," December 31, 1928, Railroad Commission of Texas files.

34. Ibid.

35. O'Neal, *Motor Busses in Texas*, pp. 27–28.
36. Joe C. Carrington, "Annual Report," p. 3.
37. "State Tour Success," pp. 6, 14.
38. Clarence E. Gilmore, "Motor Transportation," radio address delivered in San Antonio, Tex., March 28, 1929, and reprinted in *Motor Transportation in Texas*, April, 1929. See also O'Neal, *Motor Busses in Texas*, pp. 30–31, for excerpts from this important broadcast.
39. O'Neal, *Motor Busses in Texas*, p. 32.
40. Carrington interview.
41. "Annual Convention Success," p. 7.
42. Ibid.
43. J. C. Carrington to Chamber of Commerce Managers and Secretaries, June 2, 1930, my files.
44. All replies in my files.
45. J. C. Carrington to the bus operators of Texas, December 20, 1932, my files.
46. Walter H. Beck, "Address to the Third Annual Convention of the Texas Bus Owners Association," pp. 3–4.
47. Ibid.
48. "New Company to Handle Bus-Truck Insurance," p. 3.
49. "Cotton Truckers Get Injunction," p. 3.
50. "Texas Motor Transportation Association Makes Progress," pp. 5, 12.
51. "Here Is the Line-up of the New Organization," p. 6.
52. "Texans Attend the National Convention," p. 5.
53. J. C. Carrington, "Report of the Secretary-Manager of the Texas Bus Owners Association, Incorporated," September 1, 1931, my files.
54. The only female bus owner listed in Carrington's report was Mrs. A. J. Folkner, owner of the Heart of Texas Stages, Brownwood. When O'Neal went to press in 1930 with the results of his survey for *Motor Busses in Texas*, he did not mention Mrs. Folkner in the biographical sketch of her husband—yet it is her photograph, not Arthur J. Folkner's, that accompanies the sketch.

Chapter Three. The Depression and the Coming of the War

1. Jack Rhodes, "Pioneer Motorbus Operators in Texas."
2. "Bus Chatter," October, 1929, p. 18.
3. "Dixie Coaches Plan $5,000,000 Company," p. 171.
4. Ibid.
5. John P. Hoschek, "A Service Institution: Missouri Pacific Transportation Company," p. 4.
6. Theisinger, "R. C. Bowen of Texas," p. 542.
7. "Huge Merger Effected," p. 3.

8. Railroad Commission of Texas, Order by the Commission, Motor Transportation Docket #A-216, Austin, September 17, 1929, Railroad Commission of Texas files.

9. Railroad Commission of Texas, Order by the Commission, Motor Transportation Docket #A-217, Austin, September 17, 1929, Railroad Commission of Texas files.

10. "Major Cross-Country Bus Systems Form $30,000,000 Merger," p. 350.

11. "Southwestern Greyhound Lines," p. 5.

12. Schisgall, *The Greyhound Story*, p. 15.

13. "Southwestern Greyhound Lines," p. 6.

14. Ibid., p. 7.

15. Railroad Commission of Texas, Order by the Commission, Motor Transportation Docket #A-290, Austin, November 1, 1933, Railroad Commission of Texas files.

16. Guy Griggs, former president, Kerrville Bus Company, Inc., interview, Kerrville, Tex., February 14, 1980.

17. Railroad Commission of Texas, Opinion and Order by the Commission, Motor Transportation Dockets #16, #17, #18, Austin, December 3, 1927, Railroad Commission of Texas files.

18. Ibid.

19. Ibid., p. 10.

20. Griggs interview. Also, J. D. Mahaffey, former president, Kerrville Bus Company, Inc., interview, Kerrville, Tex., February 14, 1980; Henry A. Mathews, former vice-president, Kerrville Bus Company, Inc., interview, Austin, Tex., February 7, 1980.

21. Railroad Commission of Texas, Order by the Commission, Motor Transportation Division Order #A-186, Austin, March 29, 1929, Railroad Commission of Texas files.

22. Griggs and Mathews interviews.

23. Ibid. See also Thomas Urbanik II, "The Intercity Bus Industry in Texas: Problems and Potential, p. 16.

24. Hyde interview.

25. Billy H. Johnson, "Airline Motor Coaches," p. 3.

26. Ibid., pp. 5, 7.

27. Report of Airline Motor Coaches, December 31, 1935, my files.

28. Johnson, "Airline Motor Coaches," p. 9. Johnson acknowledges the cooperation of C. D. Thomas, an Airline co-founder, in his research.

29. Hyde interview. See also "G. W. Hyde," p. 12.

30. Joseph B. Eastman, "Administration of the Motor Carrier Act," p. 492.

31. Johnson, "Airline Motor Coaches," p. 7.

32. Eugene Schilder, "Motor Bus Transportation in Texas,"

unpublished report for District 7, Motor Carrier Bureau, Interstate Commerce Commission, Fort Worth, Tex., pp. 5–6, my files.

33. Theisinger, "R. C. Bowen of Texas," pp. 542–43.

34. Ibid., p. 544.

35. Handwritten account of proceedings and petitions of R. C. Bowen, my files; Hyde interview.

36. J. C. Riter, letter to Sgt. Sol Iannelli, November 10, 1943, files of the Motor Bus Society Library.

37. John P. Hoschek, "Dixie Sunshine Trailways," p. 21.

38. Schilder, "Motor Bus Transportation in Texas," pp. 1, 10, passim.

39. Hoschek, "A Service Institution," pp. 9–10.

40. Ibid., pp. 12–13. See also "National Trailways Bus System History," the 1982 special edition of *Motor Coach Age*, pp. 2–3.

41. Hyde interview.

42. Carl Stocks, "Better Times Are Just Ahead," p. 400.

43. Handwritten account of the founding and consolidation of T N M and O Coaches, files of the Motor Bus Society Library.

44. Minutes of the Meeting of the Bus Division of the Texas Motor Transportation Association, June 15, 1939, Houston, my files.

45. Ibid.

46. Ibid.

47. Minutes of the Bus Committee of the Texas Motor Transportation Association, Tyler, Tex., May 16, 1940, my files.

Chapter Four. The War and the Postwar Transition

1. A. W. Teague, Arrow Coach Lines driver, interviews, Brownwood, Tex., July 1, 1971, February 9, 1980.

2. Arthur M. Hill, "The Intercity Bus Industry," p. 46.

3. "Bus Patrons Quadrupled in D.C. Wartime Traffic," p. 84.

4. Quoted in Schisgall, *The Greyhound Story*, p. 76.

5. Carlton Jackson, *Hounds of the Road*, p. 62.

6. Albert E. Meier and John P. Hoschek, *Over the Road*, pp. 92, 94.

7. Griggs interview.

8. Johnson, "Airline Motor Coaches," p. 7.

9. J. T. McMenis, former Oklahoma Transportation Company driver, interview, Lawton, Okla., June 15, 1982.

10. Johnson, "Airline Motor Coaches," p. 7.

11. Ibid.

12. Motor Transportation Docket #A-602, Motor Trans-

portation Division, Railroad Commission of Texas, Austin, September 6, 1935, Railroad Commission of Texas files.

13. Motor Transportation Docket #A-442, Motor Transportation Division, Railroad Commission of Texas, Austin, February 9 and 13, 1933, Railroad Commission of Texas files.

14. Cofer interview.

15. Motor Carrier Docket #1643, Motor Transportation Division, Railroad Commission of Texas, Austin, January 2, 1942, Railroad Commission of Texas files.

16. Motor Transportation Docket #B-981, Motor Transportation Division, Railroad Commission of Texas, Austin, August 7, 1945, Railroad Commission of Texas files.

17. Motor Transportation Docket #B-980, Motor Transportation Division, Railroad Commission of Texas, Austin, August 23, 1945, Railroad Commission of Texas files.

18. Motor Carrier Dockets #2325-26-27-28, Motor Transportation Division, Railroad Commission of Texas, Austin, January 22, 1946, Railroad Commission of Texas files.

19. Partnership agreement for Arrow Coach Lines, March, 1946, my files.

20. John P. Hoschek, "Panhandle Trailways," pp. 20–21.

21. Interstate Commerce Commission 38-MCC-27, MC-F-1730, December 31, 1941, Interstate Commerce Commission, Washington, D.C., Interstate Commerce Commission files.

22. Interstate Commerce Commission 37-MCC-539, MC-F-1438, November 7, 1941, Interstate Commerce Commission, Washington, D.C., Interstate Commerce Commission files.

23. Interstate Commerce Commission 39-MCC-832, MC-F-1938, December 4, 1944, Interstate Commerce Commission, Washington, D.C., Interstate Commerce Commission files.

24. Interstate Commerce Commission files.

25. Interstate Commerce Commission 50-MCC-196, September 5, 1946, and November 23, 1946, Interstate Commerce Commission files.

26. Interstate Commerce Commission MC-F-3504, December 9, 1947, Interstate Commerce Commission, Washington, D.C., Interstate Commerce Commission files.

27. Hoschek, "Dixie Sunshine Trailways," p. 21.

28. Riter to Iannelli letter.

29. "Replacement Parts Restrictions Lifted," p. 7.

30. "Bus Purchases Still Restricted by ODT Order," p. 7.

31. "NAMBO Surveys Postwar Intercity Bus Needs," p. 77.

32. Hill, "The Intercity Bus Industry," p. 46.

33. Ibid.
34. "Union Bus Lines Sold—Owners Plan for Future," p. 67.
35. *Bus Transportation*, August, 1945, p. 79.
36. Motor Transportation Docket #B-1068, Motor Transportation Division, Railroad Commission of Texas, Austin, December 6, 1946, Railroad Commission of Texas files.
37. Griggs interview.
38. Ibid.
39. Johnnie J. Myers, *Texas Electric Railway*, p. 25.
40. Ibid., p. 111.
41. Ibid., p. 113.
42. Typed roster, "Those Attending Old Timers Bus Breakfast, November 5, 1956," my files.
43. Wardell Creamer to J. C. Carrington, November, 1956, my files.

Chapter Five. The Bus Lines of Oklahoma

1. Interstate Commerce Commission Docket MC-59237, Interstate Commerce Commission, Washington, D.C., November 12, 1936, Interstate Commerce Commission files.
2. Order of the Interstate Commerce Commission, Division 5, entered on the 12th day of November, A.D., 1936, Number MC-59237, Red Ball Bus Company Common Carrier Application, Interstate Commerce Commission, Washington, D.C., Interstate Commerce Commission files.
3. *Bus Transportation*, February, 1929, p. 116.
4. "Interstate Buses Topic at Oklahoma Meeting," p. 176.
5. "Oklahoma Operators Discuss Taxation," p. 118.
6. Ibid.
7. O'Neal, *Motor Busses in Texas*, p. 73.
8. "Terminal Company Elects," p. 646.
9. "Discuss Newspaper Rates at Oklahoma Meeting," p. 174.
10. Ibid. Corroborated in Carrington interview.
11. "Oklahoma Carriers Form Combined Organization," p. 159.
12. "Co-operate to Keep Down Station Expense," pp. 133–34.
13. Ibid., p. 134.
14. "Dead Mileage Eliminated by Combination Terminal-Garage," pp. 241, 242.
15. "Ward Way in Receivership," p. 637.
16. Hoschek, "Panhandle Trailways," p. 20.
17. McMenis interviews, concerning his years of experience in the bus business in Texas and Oklahoma; also J. T.

McMenis to Jack Rhodes, April 1, 1986, and November 10, 1986, my files.

18. Tom Amick, former driver, Allen's Stage Lines and M K and O Lines, interview, Tulsa, Okla., September 22, 1985.

19. Ibid. Also William P. Carson, former driver, M K and O Lines, interview, Tulsa, Okla., September 22, 1985. See also Don Stewart, "Selling a Family Business," p. C-1.

20. State of Oklahoma Certificate of Incorporation, dated September 29, 1928, Missouri Kansas and Oklahoma Lines files.

21. Interstate Commerce Commission Docket 36364, Missouri, Kansas and Oklahoma Coach Lines, 1938, Interstate Commerce Commission, Washington, D.C., Interstate Commerce Commission files.

22. Typed roster of equipment additions to Missouri Kansas and Oklahoma Coach Lines, 1938 to 1945, from data in Interstate Commerce Commission files, in the files of the Motor Bus Society Library.

23. Stewart, "Selling a Family Business," p. C-3.

24. Herbert L. Franklin, former shop foreman, M K and O Lines, interview, Tulsa, Okla., September 21, 1985; John M. Allen, assistant to the president, M K and O Lines, interview, Tulsa, Okla., September 21, 1985; Amick and Carson interviews.

25. Amick and Carson interviews.

26. "M K and O Advance Rapid in Past Year and a Half," p. 1.

27. "Oklahoma Transportation Company Sold," p. 69.

28. Amick and Carson interviews.

29. "Howard W. Allen, 63, M K & O Coach President, Dies in Plane Crash."

Chapter Six.
The Bus Lines
of New Mexico

1. Diane H. Thomas, *The Southwestern Indian Detours*, p. 42.
2. Ibid., p. 45.
3. Ibid., p. 52.
4. Ibid., p. 58.
5. Ibid., pp. 57–58.
6. Ibid., pp. 61, 63, 67, 70.
7. Ibid., pp. 70–71.
8. Robert L. Smith, "Fred Harvey," p. 15.
9. Ibid., p. 16.
10. "Santa Fe Finds Buses of Value in New Services," p. 3.
11. Ibid., p. 4.
12. "Santa Fe Tours Prove Popular," p. 1241.

13. Ibid., p. 1242.
14. Smith, "Fred Harvey," p. 17.
15. "Bus and Truck Operators Organize in Southwest," p. 358.
16. Smith, "Fred Harvey," p. 17.
17. Ibid.
18. Pat Fuqua, vice-president, New Mexico Transportation Company, interview, Roswell, N.Mex., July 25, 1983.
19. "Paul McCutchen Transportation Leader in State," p. 1; Fuqua interview.
20. "New Bus and Truck Group Formed in New Mexico," p. 691.
21. Interstate Commerce Commission Docket MC-1427, Interstate Commerce Commission, Washington, D.C., April 28, 1937, Interstate Commerce Commission files.
22. Ibid.
23. Ibid.
24. *Roswell Morning Dispatch*, May 13, 1948, p. 1.
25. Interstate Commerce Commission Docket MC-F-1477, Interstate Commerce Commission, Washington, D.C., June 27, 1941, Interstate Commerce Commission files.
26. Smith, "Fred Harvey," p. 20.
27. "650,000 Passengers Annually Carried by McCutchen Lines," p. 1.
28. "Formal Opening Saturday," p. 1.

Bibliography

Archival Materials

Barker Texas History Center, University of Texas at Austin. Austin, Tex.
Interstate Commerce Commission. Files of the Commission. Washington, D.C.
Missouri Kansas and Oklahoma Lines. Files of the Corporation. Tulsa, Okla.
Motor Bus Society Library, Motor Bus Society. West Trenton, N.J.
Railroad Commission of Texas. Files of the Motor Transportation Division. Austin, Tex.
Rhodes, Jack. Private collection. Oxford, Ohio.
Texas State Archives. Austin, Tex.

Books and Articles

"An Act to Regulate Motor Propelled Passenger Vehicles Engaged Regularly in the Business of Transporting Passengers for Hire over the Public Highways of the State of Texas; Defining Motor Bus Companies and Declaring Them Common Carriers." Chapter 270, General Laws of the Fortieth Legislature of the State of Texas, 1927.
"Annual Convention Success." *Motor Transportation in Texas*, May, 1929, pp. 7, 11.
Beck, Walter H. "Address to the Third Annual Convention of the Texas Bus Owners Association." *Motor Transportation*, July, 1931, pp. 3-4.
"Bus and Truck Operators Organize in Southwest." *Bus Transportation*, June, 1929, p. 358.
"Bus Chatter." *Motor Transportation*, October, 1929, p. 18; September, 1930, p. 22.
Bush, Donald J. *The Streamlined Decade*. New York: George Braziller, 1975.
"Bus Patrons Quadrupled in D.C. Wartime Traffic." *Bus Transportation*, October, 1945, p. 84.
"Bus Purchases Still Restricted by ODT Order." *Bus Transportation*, July, 1945, p. 7.
Bus Transportation, February, 1929, p. 116; August, 1945, p. 79.

Carrington, Joe C. "Annual Report." *Motor Transportation in Texas*, April, 1929, pp. 3–4.

Cizek, Hazel Crosby. "'What! No Towels?' The Theme Song of the Bus Traveler." *Bus Transportation*, January, 1935, pp. 3–6.

"Co-operate to Keep Down Station Expense." *Bus Transportation*, March, 1930, pp. 132–35.

"Cotton Truckers Get Injunction." *Motor Transportation*, August, 1931, p. 3.

"Dead Mileage Eliminated by Combination Terminal-Garage." *Bus Transportation*, May, 1930, pp. 241–43.

"Discuss Newspaper Rates at Oklahoma Meeting." *Bus Transportation*, March, 1930, p. 174.

"Dixie Coaches Plan $5,000,000 Company." *Bus Transportation*, March, 1929, p. 171.

Eastman, Joseph B. "Administration of the Motor Carrier Act." *Bus Transportation*, November, 1935, pp. 492–93.

"Formal Opening Saturday." *Roswell Morning Dispatch*, May 13, 1948, p. 1.

Fuller, Wayne E. *RFD: The Changing Face of Rural America*. Bloomington: Indiana University Press, 1964.

"G. W. Hyde: Success Story—Central Texas Bus Line." *Bowen Trailway News*, February, 1945, pp. 10–12.

Gilmore, Clarence E. "Motor Transportation." *Motor Transportation in Texas*, April, 1929.

"Here Is the Line-up of the New Organization." *Motor Transportation*, July, 1932, p. 6.

Hill, Arthur M. "The Intercity Bus Industry." *Bus Transportation*, September, 1945, p. 46.

Hoschek, John P. "Dixie Sunshine Trailways." *Motor Coach Age*, June, 1968, pp. 20–22.

———. "Panhandle Trailways." *Motor Coach Age*, December, 1984, pp. 20–23.

———. "A Service Institution: Missouri Pacific Transportation Company." *Motor Coach Age*, October, 1976, pp. 4–22.

"Howard W. Allen, 63, M K & O Coach President, Dies in Plane Crash." *Tulsa Tribune*, February 28, 1964.

"Huge Merger Effected." *Motor Transportation in Texas*, October, 1929, pp. 3–4.

"Interstate Buses Topic at Oklahoma Meeting." *Bus Transportation*, March, 1928, p. 176.

"Inventors to Honor Forgotten Man." *Buffalo Evening News*, September 3, 1935.

Jackson, Carlton. *Hounds of the Road*. Bowling Green, Ohio: Bowling Green Popular University Press, 1984.

Johnson, Billy H. "Airline Motor Coaches." *Bus History*, January–March, 1975, pp. 3–9.
"Made to Make You Money." *Motor Coach Age*, March, 1969, pp. 4–20.
"Major Cross-Country Bus Systems Form $30,000,000 Merger." *Bus Transportation*, June, 1929, pp. 350–52.
Meier, Albert E., and John P. Hoschek. *Over the Road*. Trenton, N.J.: Motor Bus Society, 1975.
"M K and O Advance Rapid in Past Year and a Half." *Riding the Trails with Trailways*, May, 1937, p. 1.
Moore, Walter B. "Preachers Warned against First Texas Bus." *Dallas Morning News*, February 13, 1970.
Myers, Johnnie J. *Texas Electric Railway*. Chicago: Central Electric Railfans Association, 1982.
"NAMBO Surveys Postwar Intercity Bus Needs." *Bus Transportation*, January, 1945, p. 77.
"National Trailways Bus System History." *Motor Coach Age*, Special Issue, 1982.
"New Bus and Truck Group Formed in New Mexico." *Bus Transportation*, December, 1930, p. 691.
"New Company to Handle Bus-Truck Insurance." *Motor Transportation*, August, 1931, p. 3.
"Oklahoma Carriers Form Combined Organization." *Bus Transportation*, March, 1931, p. 159.
"Oklahoma Operators Discuss Taxation." *Bus Transportation*, February, 1929, p. 118.
"Oklahoma Transportation Company Sold." *Bus Transportation*, July, 1945, p. 69.
O'Neal, Wendell. *Motor Busses in Texas 1912–1930*. Austin: Texas Bus Owners Association, [1930].
"Paul McCutchen Transportation Leader in State." *Roswell Morning Dispatch*, May 13, 1948, p. 1.
"Replacement Parts Restrictions Lifted." *Bus Transportation*, July, 1945, p. 7.
Rhodes, Jack. "Pioneer Motorbus Operators in Texas." Paper presented at the Texas State Historical Association meeting, El Paso, Tex., 1981.
———. "Still 'Loading Passengers in Lane One': Texas' Independent Bus Lines." *Dallas Times Herald Sunday Magazine*, January 9, 1972, p. 12.
Riding the Trails with Trailways, May, 1937, pp. 1–4.
Roswell Morning Dispatch, May 13, 1948, p. 1.
"Santa Fe Finds Buses of Value in New Services." *Bus Transportation*, January, 1927, pp. 1–4.
"Santa Fe Tours Prove Popular." *Railway Age*, May 26, 1928, pp. 1241–44.

Schisgall, Oscar. *The Greyhound Story: From Hibbing to Everywhere*. Chicago: J. G. Ferguson Publishing Company, 1985.

Simon, Leonard G. "The Start of America's Amazing Bus Industry." In *Lore and Legend: A Compilation of Documents Depicting the History of Colorado City and Mitchell County*, compiled by Mac B. McKinnon. 2 vols. Colorado City, Tex.: Colorado City Record Publishers, 1975.

———. "Texas' First Bus Run: 30 Miles in 12 Hours." *Texas Highways*, July, 1975, pp. 27–28.

"650,000 Passengers Annually Carried by McCutchen Lines." *Roswell Morning Dispatch*, May 13, 1948, pp. 1–2.

Smith, Robert L. "Fred Harvey." *Motor Coach Age*, August–September, 1983, pp. 4–34.

"Southwestern Greyhound Lines." *Motor Coach Age*, December, 1967, pp. 4–8.

"State Tour Success." *Motor Transportation in Texas*, April, 1929, pp. 6, 14.

Steward, Don. "Selling a Family Business." *Tulsa Tribune*, October 9, 1986, pp. C-1, C-3.

Stocks, Carl. "Better Times Are Just Ahead." *Bus Transportation*, June, 1930, p. 400.

"Terminal Company Elects." *Bus Transportation*, November, 1929, p. 646.

"Texans Attend the National Convention." *Motor Transportation*, October, 1931, p. 5.

"Texas Motor Transportation Association Makes Progress." *Motor Transportation*, July, 1932, pp. 5, 12.

"Texas Pioneers in Transportation." *San Antonio Express/News*, June 27, 1971.

Theisinger, Earl F. "R. C. Bowen of Texas." *Bus Transportation*, December 15, 1935, pp. 541–45.

Thomas, Diane H. *The Southwestern Indian Detours*. Phoenix, Ariz.: Hunter Publishing Company, 1978.

"Truck Men to Honor Pioneer." *Dallas Times Herald*, May 21, 1941, p. 12.

"Union Bus Lines Sold—Owners Plan for Future." *Bus Transportation*, March, 1945, p. 67.

Urbanik, Thomas, II. "The Intercity Bus Industry in Texas: Problems and Potential." Ph.D. dissertation, Texas A&M University, 1982.

"Ward Way in Receivership." *Bus Transportation*, November, 1930, p. 637.

"We Mourn." *Motor Transportation*, September, 1930, p. 3.

BIBLIOGRAPHY

Interviews

Allen, John M., assistant to the president, M K and O Lines. Tulsa, Okla., September 21, 1985.

Amick, Tom, former driver, Allen's Stage Lines and M K and O Lines. Tulsa, Okla., September 22, 1985.

Carrington, Joe C., former secretary/manager, Texas Bus Owners Association. Austin, Tex., February, 1980.

Carson, William P., former driver, M K and O Lines. Tulsa, Okla., September 22, 1985.

Cofer, Alice Roberson, former owner, Arrow Coach Lines. Lampasas, Tex., February 8, 1980.

Franklin, Herbert L., former shop foreman, M K and O Lines. Tulsa, Okla., September 21, 1985.

Fuqua, Pat, vice-president, New Mexico Transportation Company. Roswell, N.Mex., July 25, 1983.

Griggs, Guy, former president, Kerrville Bus Company, Inc. Kerrville, Tex., February 14, 1980.

Hyde, G. W., founder of Central Texas Bus Lines. Cleburne, Tex., February 20, 1980.

McMenis, J. T., former driver and ticket agent for Oklahoma Transportation Company. Lawton, Okla., 1954–86, esp. June 15, 1982.

Mahaffey, J. D., former president, Kerrville Bus Company, Inc. Kerrville, Tex., February 14, 1980.

Mathews, Henry A., former vice-president, Kerrville Bus Company, Inc. Austin, Tex., February 7, 1980.

Murphey, W. L., co-owner and president, Sun Set Stages. Abilene, Tex., June 30, 1971.

Murphey, Bill R., Mary, Pat, and Sue, family owners and operators of Sun Set Stages. Abilene, Tex., January–February, 1980.

Shearer, Gladys McCarty, secretary to Joe C. Carrington. Austin, Tex., 1980–85.

Teague, A. W., driver, Arrow Coach Lines. Brownwood, Tex., July 1, 1971, and February 9, 1980.

Index

Italicized numbers indicate that the item appears in a picture caption.

Abbott, Ed, 8–9, 11, 45, 97
Abilene–San Angelo Coaches, 89
Adams, Mrs. Alex, 35
airline connections, 46
Airline Motor Coaches: and Beck buses during wartime, 75; company report of, for 1935, 56–57; formation of, 55; history and development of, 55–57; ICC approval of intrastate route for, 59–60; importance of, in 1936 report, 62; sold to Dixie-Sunshine Trailways, 56; staff ca. 1936, *59*; and TMTA Bus Division, 66; Trailways network participation of, 83; wartime passenger loads of, 75
Alderman, John, 34
Allen, Howard Wesley: accidental death of, 117; affiliates with Trailways, 111; and Allen's Motor Lines, 109; at Cushing in 1928, *104*; buys out Spurgin interests, 113; dedication of employees of, 113–14; dedication of, to bus company, 113–14; early career of, 108–109; as founder of M K and O Lines, *101*; incorporates M K and O Lines, 109–10; moves bus line to Cushing, 109; as president of M K and O Lines, 114; recalled as Oklahoma pioneer, 134; Wichita operations of, *101*, *102*, 108–109
Allen, M. L. (Mrs. Howard Wesley), 110

Allen, Robert, 117
Allen's Auto Stage Line (Allen's Motor Lines), *102*, 109–10
Amarillo-Denver Bus Company, 80–81
Amberson, James, 53, 90
Amberson, Joe: as charter member of TBOA, 22; enters Trailways network, 83; forms Union Bus Lines, 53; sells lines to Mann and Mabry, 86
American Car Foundry, 66, *82*, *90*
Amick, Tom, *111*
Amtrak, 133
Anderson, Andy, 7
Arrow Coach Lines: Camp Bowie service, 70, 72, *76*; clipboard map for, *78*; convergence of, routes at Brownwood, 76; Flxible coach in 1944, *72*; general postwar expansion of, 89; and oral partnership agreement, 76; origin of, 10, 76; postwar development of, 78–79; postwar ownership of, 79; secures rights to Camp Hood, 78; tractor-trailer buses, 83; troop movements by, 77; World War II role of, 76–77
Atascosa Bus Lines, 92
Austin, Mrs. E. L., 35
Austin Chamber of Commerce, 43–44
Awtry, John H., 43

Baldwin Motor Company, *12*
Ballinger, Texas: main street of, *11*

INDEX

Bankhead, John, 8
Barrett, A. P., 46
Barrett, A. T.: as guest of Oklahoma Bus and Truck Operators, 102; as head of Motor Carrier Insurance Agency, 41; leadership of, 44; as president of TBOA, 37; retires, 43
Bay Shore Bus Line, 65
Beaumont-Port Arthur Bus Line, 65, 68
Beck, C. D., 74
Beck, Walter H.: addresses first TBOA convention, 35; addresses third TBOA convention, 39–41; leadership of, 44; as officer of TMTA, 42; warns TBOA and TTOA against railroads, 40–41; writes Motor Bus Law, 15
Beck Bus Law (Motor Bus Law), 15, 16–18, 24, 29, 35, 52
Beck Company, 74–75, 76, 86, 88
Bee Line Coaches, 58, 62, 66
Belcher, R(ayner) M(elton), 76–77, 79
Belcher, Robert, 79
Bell, Bryan, 41, 94
Bender, C. J., 12
B. F. Goodrich Company, 94
Bill's Bus Line, 55
Black, W. J., 118
Black and White Lines, 100, 110
Black Diamond Lines, 13
Bogan, Ralph, 49
Bowen, R. C., 21, 45, 97; and Amarillo-Denver Bus Company, 80–81; assists Southland transition, 48; and Breckenridge oilfields, 21; chairs Bus Division of TMTA, 66; consolidates lines in 1937– 38, 60–61; and Continental Bus System, 81–83; and Great Depression, 65; interviewed in *Bus Transportation*, 60; leadership of, 44; makes lease with J. S. Folkner, 79; and Lone Star Coaches, Inc., 79–82; moves into Trailways system, 82–83; opinions of, on Bus Divi-

Bowen, R. C. (cont.)
sion matters, 67–68; passenger service policies of, 60; and postwar system expansion, 89; purchases Creamer Stage Line, 62; rebuilds rival route system, 60; sells interests to Southland-Red Ball, 47–49; and South Texas Coaches, 21; supports Motor Carrier Act, 60; and TBOA, 18–22, 23, 26; and T N M and O Coaches, 65–66; and wartime expansion, 79–81
Bowen Motor Coaches: Beck buses used by, during war, 75–76, 76; Camp Bowie service, 70; commuter service, 81; and Continental Bus System, 81–83; and fatal bus accident, 80; bus interior, 82; sold to Trailways, 61; standing in 1936 report, 62; statistics for 1935-36, 60; stock sale to Lone Star Coaches, 79–80; and TMTA Bus Division, 66; tractor-trailer buses of, 83–84, 84
Bowers, Robert S., 115
Bowman, Joe, 66
Brownwood-Brady Bus Line, 79
Brenham, Texas: bus station at, 88
Buick buses, 4, 128
Burlington Railroad (C B and Q RR), 64
Burris, Ed C., 38
Burt, H. L., 22–23, 27

Caesar, Orville S., 49
Camp Bowie, Texas, 70, 72, 76, 79, 83, 84, 93
Canuteson, Sam, 57, 64
Carrington, Joe C., 36, 36, 37–39; and Code of Ethics, 27–28; and Cuero Chamber of Commerce, 24, 25, 37; elected to Texas legislature, 95; as guest of Oklahoma Bus and Truck Operators, 102; hosts "Old Timers Bus Breakfasts," 93–97; leadership of, 44; letter of appointment for, 25; and

Carrington, Joe C. (cont.)
  Motor Carrier Insurance Agency, 41; remembers Sam Johnson, 34; and report of September 1, 1931, 43–44; responsibilities of, in 1931, 41; as secretary of TMTA, 42; and "Suggested Plan of Work," 26; and TBOA, 23–24, 30, 32, 34–35; and wildcatters, 29
Carson, William P. ("Pinky"), 106, 112
Central Texas Bus Lines, 57–58, 62, 71
Certificates of Convenience and Necessity, 16–17
Chenoweth, W. B., 3–4, 4, 5, 6, 45, 97; and Beck Bus Law protections, 15
Chisholm Trail Stages, 90, 92
Chrysler Corporation buses, 55, 84
Clanton, B. H., 103
Clarkson, R. Hunter: and Ford Harvey, 118–21; incorporates, 125; and Indian Detours, 118–20, 125, 132; intervenes against New Mexico Transportation Company, 129–30; limits service to Lamy–Santa Fe only, 126; orders coaches with special features, 121; receives Lamy–Santa Fe concession from ICC, 129–30; sells Albuquerque–Santa Fe rights to Frank McCutchen, 128
Cleburne–Fort Worth Motor Coaches, 58, 71
Clifford, F. N., 30
Cofer, Alice Roberson, 79, 94–95
commuter operations, 65–68, 68, 74, 81
Continental Bus System, 81–83
Continental Trailways, 82–83, 110–12, 115, 117
Cook, L. L., 90
Cooper, Tom, 101, 108, 114–15
Cotton Belt Railroad, 12, 32, 47, 50, 92
Creamer, B. G., 89–90, 96
Creamer, J. C., 96
Creamer, Louis Hardy, 7–8, 45, 62, 78, 82–83, 96

Creamer, Wardell, 96
Creamer Stage Line, 7, 62, 82–83
Cuero Chamber of Commerce, 24, 25, 37

Dallas–Wichita Falls Coaches, 61
Day, Sam, 45; and Bee Line Coaches, 58; and Code of Ethics, 27; leadership of, 44; regrets missing "Old Timers Bus Breakfast," 95; and TBOA, 22, 23, 29
DeBerry, C. B., 43
Denison and Sherman Railway Company, 91
Dixie Motor Coaches, 47, 56–57, 61–62
Dixie Sunshine Trailways, 61–62, 70, 83, 89
Duvall, J. C., 15, 23–24, 32, 37, 44, 57

Eckstrom, Edward C., 47–48, 49–50, 95
Edwards, J. H., 34
English, Clarence T., 55
English, Henry, 95

Fageol buses, 9
Faulkner, Dean M., 106–107
Faulkner, Ward, 100–101, 105–107
Firestone Tire and Rubber Company, 94
first intercity bus in Texas, 3–4
Fite and Wallace Bus Line, 55
Fitzjohn sedans, 54
Flxible Corporation buses, 71, 72, 77, 87, 89, 91, 93, 94, 112, 114, 115, 132
Folkner, J. S., 79
Ford, William, 41
Fort Hood, Texas (Camp Hood), 77, 78, 93
Fort Sill, Oklahoma, 117
Fred Harvey Company, 118, 120–21, 125
Freeman, Fred, 22, 45
Freeman, W. E., 11

Galveston and Houston Auto Transportation Company, 9
Gamble, (Judge), 24

INDEX

General American Aerocoach Company, 116
General Motors Corporation, 73
Giles, Carl, 100–101
Gilmore, Clarence E., 32–33, 44, 48
Glisson, H. S., 30, 37
Good Roads Movement, 8
Great Depression: emergence from, 69; and Oklahoma bus industry, 105–107, 117; and Texas bus industry, 64–65
Greer, Webb, 65
Greyhound Lines: air-to-bus transfers, 46; allies with Kerrville Bus Company, 50, 54; and coast-to-coast merger, 49; founding of, 7; and the "Greyhound of the Highways," 20, 47; "Nite Coach" service of, 51; Painter Bus Lines hood ornament of, 58; suppliers of, during wartime, 73; through service in New Mexico, 130; through service in Oklahoma, 117; and wartime maintenance problems, 73. *See also* Southland Greyhound Lines; Southwestern Greyhound Lines
Griggs, Guy, 53, 68, 95, 96, 134
Gulf Oil Corporation, 27
Guthrie, J. E., 38

Hancock, Robert W., 88
Hannan, Charles, M., 22–24
Harvey, Byron, 125
Harvey, Ford, 118, 120, 125
Harvey, Fred, 118
Harvey, Frederick, 120–21
Hawkins, C. D., 30
Hays, Nat, 29
Heket, Dutch, 82, 107
Hickox, R. G., 99–101
Highway Act of 1916, 8
highway conditions: from Cushing to Tulsa in 1925, 109; and Good Roads Movement, 8; on Kerrville Bus Company routes, 53; in wartime, 72–73, 113; on W. B. Chenoweth's route, 3–5

Hill, Arthur M., 84–86
Hill, Charles, 125
Hooker, H. O., 59
Houston, Humble, and Livingston Bus Line, 55
Hyde, George Wellington ("Bill"), 12–13, 45, 55, 57, 58, 64–65, 71, 94

Indian Detours: beginnings of, 118, 123; in compliance with Motor Transportation Division, 124; described, 119–20; development and operation of, 118–26; equipment of, 119–22, 126; and Hunter Clarkson, 118–20; name of, sold to Frank McCutchen, 133; postwar recovery of, 131–32; profit picture of, 125; reduced to Lamy–Santa Fe only, 126; and Santa Fe Transportation Company, 123–24; suspended by ODT, 126
Inter City Transit Lines, 126, 127, 128
Interstate Commerce Commission (ICC), 6, 15, 58–60, 63–64, 67, 81–82, 128–30

Jacobson, Grover C., 103
Jasper Chamber of Commerce, 38
J. H. McLeaish Trucking Company, 42
Johnson, B. Frank, 67
Johnson, Sam, 34
Jones, Tom, 42
Jordan, B. G., 107
Jordan, Eugene, 115
Jordan, Julia, 115
Jordan Bus Company, 107, 115, 117

Katy Railroad (Missouri-Kansas-Texas Railroad Company), 6
Kemp, John, 79
Kemp Bus Lines, 79, 92, 93
Kenworth buses, 126
Kerrville Bus Company, Incorporated: acquires Merritt franchises, 6, 53–54; allies with Greyhound, 50, 54; and Austin-Houston ser-

INDEX

Kerrville Bus Company (cont.) vices, 56; and Beck Company arrangements, 74–75; in Great Depression, 65; Hal Peterson ownership of, 51–53; and highway conditions, 53; history and development of, 50–54; in 1936 report, 62; passengers in Austin, 57; postwar designs of, 86, 88; and postwar routes, 89–90; purchases Painter Bus Lines, 54; and Railroad Commission dispute, 51–53; and Ross Motor Coaches, 77; and TMTA Bus Division, 67
Killion, Mrs. M. O., 79
Knutson, J. A., 35

Littlefield Building (Austin, Texas), 39, 41

Mabry, L. R., 86, 89
McCallum, James Y., 22
McCoy, R. R., 100
McCutchen, Frank, 126, 128, 131, 133
McCutchen, Paul, 127, 128, 128, 129–31, 133–34
McKenzie, M. A., 102
McKissick, Robert, 89
Mack's Motor Coaches, 67
McMakin, Grover C., 65, 126–27
McMakin Motor Coaches, 62, 65, 126–27
McNally, Carl, 127, 129
Mahaffey, J. D., 53
Majors, B. H., 88
Mann, Guy J., 86–89
Marshall, Mark: cited for cooperation by TBOA, 32; on Glacier National Park tour, 36; on "Good Will and Education Tour," 32; leadership of, 44; and Motor Transportation Division, 15, 17–18; recalled as pioneer, 97
Mathews, Henry A., 53
Mehew, Charles E., 100–101, 103
Merritt, G. J. ("Josh"), 6, 45, 54
Mesaba Transportation Company, 7

Mid-Continent Coaches, 108, 115
Missouri Pacific Railroad, 6, 47, 64, 92
Missouri Pacific Transportation Company, 40, 47, 48, 62, 63, 63–64
"Miss Texas," 44
M K and O Lines (Missouri, Kansas, and Oklahoma Lines, Incorporated): ad poster, 109; affiliates with Trailways, 110, 110–12; equipment in 1929, 107; founding of, 108–10; and Howard Wesley Allen, 101; incorporates, 109–10; merges with Black and White Lines, 101; and Oklahoma A&M class trip, 105; postwar condition of, 116–17; Reo buses of, in Oklahoma City, 103; and report of 1938 to ICC, 110–11; and route structure in 1928, 110; shop operations of, 111–12; during World War II, 111–13; staff, 104, 106
Monzingo Bus Lines, 56
Moody, Governor (Dan), 33
Mooney Motor coaches, 92, 94
Moore, M. E., 81–82
Motor Bus Law. See Beck Bus Law
Motor Carrier Act of 1935, 59
Motor Carrier Insurance Agency, 41
Motor Carriers Association of New Mexico, 128
Motor Carriers of Oklahoma, 103–104
Motor Transportation, 37, 41–43
Motor Transportation Department (New Mexico), 124
Motor Transportation Division (Texas): certificates and franchises, 16–17; established by RCT, 15; first report of, 17–18; inspectors appointed for, 34; and Motor Carrier Act of 1935, 58–59; and Rule 35, 24; second report of, 31; and stewardship of Mark Marshall, 15, 97. *See also* Rail-

INDEX

Motor Trans. Division (cont.)
 road Commission of Texas
 (RCT)
*Motor Transportation in
 Texas,* 28, 30, 37
Murphey, O. C., 11, 45
Murphey, Sue, 89
Murphey, W. L., 11, 89, 97

National Association of Motor
 Bus Owners (NAMBO), 43,
 84–86
National Engineering Laboratory, 3
National Motor Bus Clergy
 Bureau, 39
National Safety Council, 43
National Trailways Bus System, 63–64
Neff, Pat, 33, 44
Neff, Paul J., 64
Nelson, (Judge), 24
New Mexico Military Institute, *130*
New Mexico Motorways, 123
New Mexico Transportation
 Company, 127–28, 129–31,
 131, 132, 133, 133–34
New Mexico Truck and Bus
 Owners Association, 125
Northland Transportation
 Company, 49
Nunnelee, Walter E.: and Certificate Number One, 11;
 as charter member of
 TBOA, 22; fleet in Tyler,
 12; inaugurates Tyler-
 Longview-Marshall bus service, 11; moves to hire Joe
 C. Carrington, 24; sells
 bus interests to Cotton
 Belt, 12, 32, 45, 50

Office of Defense Transportation (ODT): curtails routes,
 70; provides for meetings
 of bus operators, 73; relaxes wartime restrictions,
 83–84; requisitions buses,
 70–71; suspends Indian
 Detours, 126
Office of Public Road Inquiry,
 8
oil fields (Texas), 8
Oklahoma Motor Bus and
 Truck Operators Association, 98–102, 103

Oklahoma Railway Company,
 115
Oklahoma Transportation
 Company, 100–101, 104–
 107, *114, 115,* 116–17
"Old Timers Bus Breakfasts,"
 93–97
O'Neal, Wendell, 30, 32

Page, H. T., 127, 130
Page-Way Stage Lines, Incorporated (Page-Way System),
 127, 130
Painter, Allura, 54
Painter, Walter R., 45, 54, 97
Painter Bus Lines, 54, *58,* 62,
 75, *91*
Panhandle Stages (Panhandle
 Motor Coaches), 62, 66–67,
 79, 82, 107
Parks, Howard, 22–23, 29
Parrish, Fred, 125–26
Parrish Stage Line, 125–26
Patterson, Moss: as director of
 TBOA, 102; early career of,
 100; and Great Depression,
 107–108; and Oklahoma
 Transportation Company,
 100, 104–105, 114; as president of Mid-Continent
 Trailways, 115; as president
 of Motor Carriers of Oklahoma, 103; as president of
 Oklahoma Bus and Truck
 Association, 101; as president of Oklahoma City
 Bus Terminal Association,
 100–101; regrets missing
 "Old Timers Bus Breakfast," 95
Pendleton, Miller, 53
Peterson, Hal, 51–53, 68, 74,
 97
Phillips Petroleum Company,
 94
Pickwick Greyhound Lines
 (Pickwick Stages), 46, 49,
 51
Pine, W. E., *35*
Pollard, Claude, 29
postwar period, transitions in,
 83–86; cessation of lines
 and service, 92–93; decline
 in ridership, 92; passenger
 car competition, 85, 92;
 passenger resistance to
 buses, 85–87; economic

postwar period (*cont.*)
  optimism, 84–85, 88; public accommodations, 86–87; in Texas, 86–97
Power, J. A., 51–53, 97
Power, J. L., 51–53, 97
public relations, 85–89
Puterbaugh, J. G., 106

Railroad Commission of Texas (RCT), 15, 23–24, 31–32, 33, 91
railroads: and declining passenger revenues, 90; and formation of highway subsidiaries, 47; influence of, on coach design, *40*; and Josh Merritt, 6; as link for bus lines, 5; perceived as "enemy," 39–41; and Texas Electric Bus Lines, 90–92; and Texas Electric Railway, 90–91
Rainbow Coaches, 92, 108, 115
Red Ball Bus Company (Red Ball Bus and Baggage Company of Oklahoma), 98–100, 107, 115
Red Ball Stage Line (Texas), 13, 55
Red Star Coaches (of Vernon), 62
Red Star Lines, 13, 55
Reo buses, *101*, *103*, *105*, *107*
Riter, A. W., 43, 62
Riter, J. C., 61–62
Roberson, A. V., 10
Roberson, Clarence E.: clipboard map of, *78*; early oilfield operations of, 9–11; estate of, 79; and nucleus of Arrow Coach Lines, 10, 76–77; Stephenville–Fort Worth service of, 10
Roberson Bus Lines, 38–39
Robertson, Robert L., 29
Rocksprings Motor Coaches, 92
Ross, B. U., 76–79
Ross, Edgar, 100
Ross Motor Coaches, 77
Roswell-Alamogordo Stage, *128*

Salado Chamber of Commerce, 38

San Antonio, Texas: bus terminal at, 32, *33*, *34*, *35*
Santa Fe Chamber of Commerce, 119
Santa Fe Railway (Atchison, Topeka, and Santa Fe Railway Company): arranges for Indian Detours, 118–21; cooperates with Hunter Clarkson, 125; and discussions with Burlington and Missouri Pacific, 64; and highway subsidiaries in Texas, 47, 92; intervenes against New Mexico Transportation Company, 129–30; reclaims Indian Detours from Clarkson, 132–33; and Santa Fe Transportation Company, 123–24
Santa Fe Trail Stages, 99, *113*
Santa Fe Transportation Company, 123–24
Shackleford, Dorsey, 8
Shearer, Gladys McCarty, 30, 94
Shields, Guy J., 19, 44; and Southland Greyhound, 48; and Southland–Red Ball Motor Bus Company, 18–19; and TBOA, 18, 22, 23, 24–25, *25*
Shirley, J. E., 120–21
Short, George, 37
Sledz, Adam, 73
Smith, Lon, 33, 44, 48, 50
Southern Kansas Stage Lines, 99
Southern Pacific Railroad, 6, 49, 92, 129
Southern Traction Company, 90
Southland Greyhound Lines: becomes Southwestern Greyhound Lines, 50; formation of, 47; initial route structure of, 49; and merger, 48–49. *See also* Greyhound Lines; Southland–Red Ball Motor Bus Company; Southwestern Greyhound Lines
Southland–Red Ball Motor Bus Company: acquires Bowen interests, 47–48; advertising in *Texas Commercial News*, *20*; and new San Antonio terminal, 33;

Southland–Red Ball Co. (cont.) building coach in garage of, 27; coach and driver of, 19; departing new San Antonio terminal, 34; and involvement of Edward C. Eckstrom, 49–50; and involvement of Guy J. Shields, 18–19; and Red Ball Bus and Baggage Company, 98; and San Antonio socialites, 35. See also Southwestern Greyhound Lines
South Plains Coaches, 65
South Texas Coaches, 18, 21, 47, 62
Southwest Coaches, 115
Southwestern Greyhound Lines: formation and acquisitions of, 50; influence of, in Texas, 50, 62; and Kemp Bus Lines, 79; and New Mexico Transportation Company, 130–31; in Oklahoma, 116; role of Paul W. Tibbetts in, 134; and takeover bid for Oklahoma Transportation Company, 130–31; and TMTA Bus Division, 66
Southwestern Transportation Company, 32, 43, 50
Spurgin, A. S. (Mrs. J. Will), 110
Spurgin, J. Will, 100–101, 103, 106, 110
State Corporation Commission (New Mexico), 124
State Corporation Commission (Oklahoma), 99–100
statistics: on Airline Motor coaches, 56–57; on Bowen Motor coaches, 60; on Dixie-Sunshine for 1942–43, 83; on formation of Dixie Motor Coaches, 47; on formation of Southland Greyhound Lines, 47; on Missouri Pacific bus operations, 47; in M K and O Lines report to ICC, 110–11; on New Mexico Transportation Company as of 1948, 133–34; on Oklahoma Transportation Company 1928–30, 105; in reports of Motor Transporta-

statistics (cont.) tion Division, 18, 31; on Santa Fe Transportation Company, 124; on Ward Way system, 106
Steffan, P. A., 125
Stephenville Chamber of Commerce, 38–39
Stocks, Carl, 64–65
Stockton, Colonel J. T., 24
streamlining, 54, 55, 61
Studebaker buses, 12, 13, 48, 63, 107
Sun Set Stages, 11
Sunshine Bus Lines, 55, 61–62
Superior Coach Company, 127

Talley, O. L., 38–39
Terrell, C. V., 33, 35, 44, 48, 50
Texas Air Transport, 46
Texas Bus Lines: city-style bus of, 74; commuter success of, 65–66, 66; "Miss Texas" model of, 44; and TMTA Bus Division, 66
Texas Bus Owners Association: accomplishments of, in 1928, 30; affiliations of, 43–44; board meetings of, 22–28; and chambers of commerce, 37–38; charter of, 22; and Code of Ethics, 27–28; cooperates with RCT, 31–33; at Glacier National Park conference, 33, 36; individuals involved in, 23, 24, 93–97; incorporates, 22; initial leaders of, 18–21; need for, 18; and railroad competition, 39–41; and role of Bus Division under TMTA, 66–69; routine business of, 26; supports trucker's injunction, 42; and wildcatters, 29
Texas Commercial Executives Association, 37, 43
Texas Electric Bus Lines, 90–92
Texas Electric Railway, 90–91
Texas Motorcoaches, 65, 67, 88, 90
Texas Motor Transportation Association (TMTA), 39–43, 66–69, 93

Texas Oil, *10*, 27
Texas Traction Company, 90
Texas Trade Executive Association, 43
Texas Truck Owners Association (TTOA), 37, 39, 41–43
Texas Wagon Works, 10
Thomas, C. D., 55, *59*, 69, 95
Thomas Motor Coaches, 55
Thompson, Ernest O., 50
Thompson, J. J., 22
Tibbetts, Paul W., *35*, 43, 134
Tinker Air Force Base (Oklahoma), 117
T N M and O Coaches, Incorporated (Texas, New Mexico, and Oklahoma Coaches), 65–66, *87*, 89
Toliver, (Dillard A.), 93
Transcontinental Bus System (Continental Trailways), 82–83
"travel bureaus," 68–69
Tulsa, Oklahoma: bus terminal at, *108*
Twin Coach buses, 67

Union Bus Company, 51–53, 97
Union Bus Lines, 53, *54*, *55*, 62, 83, 86
United States Chamber of Commerce, 43
United States Good Roads Association, 43
Utecht, Jack, 23–24

Veal, P. R. ("Speedy"), 11

Wallace, Guy, 125
Walters, O. E., 34
Ward Way Coaches, 100, 105–108

War Production Board, 70, 74
Weicker, R. A., 103
W. E. Nunnelee Auto Line, 11, *12*, *13*, 32
Western Air Express, 46
West Texas Coaches, *11*, 47
White, W. S., 22
White Company buses, 61, 74, 81, *107*, *109*, 119, 120, 121, 122, 123, *131*
White Line Stage Company, *127*, *129*
Wichita Carriage Works, 102
Wickman, Carl Eric, 7, 49
wildcatting, 13–14, 16, 28–30, 45
Will buses (C. H. Will Motor Coach Corporation), *19*, 36
Williams, R. L., 106
Williamson, Charlie, 30
Wilson, Woodrow, 8
Woodlief, W. H., 80–81
World War II: Beck Company bus production in, 74–75; bus operating conditions during, 70–74, 75, 79, 83; bus travel statistics during, 71; effect of, on Indian Detours, 125–26; effect of, on Oklahoma bus lines, 111–13; military establishments in Texas during, 70–71, 76; overcrowding of vehicles during, 70–72, 75–76
Wren, M. S., 48

Yelloway system, 49
Yellow Coach Company, *110*, 120–21, 123
Young, Hugo, 87
Young's Bus Line, 47

Intercity Bus Lines of the Southwest was composed into type on a Compugraphic digital phototypesetter in nine and one-half point Trump Medieval with two and one-half point spacing between the lines. Friz Quadrata was selected for title page display. The book was designed by Jim Billingsley, typeset by Metricomp, Inc., printed offset by Thomson-Shore, Inc., and bound by John H. Dekker & Sons. The paper on which the book is printed is designed for an effective life of at least three hundred years.

TEXAS A&M UNIVERSITY PRESS : COLLEGE STATION

www.ingramcontent.com/pod-product-compliance
Lightning Source LLC
Chambersburg PA
CBHW030324080526
44584CB00012B/703